MW01000204

CELEBRATING THE
RITES OF INITIATION

CELEBRATING THE
RITES OF INITIATION

A Practical Ceremonial Guide
for Clergy and Other Liturgical Ministers

James F. Turrell

Church Publishing
NEW YORK

© 2013 by James F. Turrell
All rights reserved.

Library of Congress Cataloging-in-Publication Data

A catalog record of this book is available from the Library of Congress.

ISBN-13: 978-0-89869-875-6 (pbk.)
ISBN-13: 978-0-89869-876-3 (ebook)

Cover design by Laurie Klein Westhafer
Typeset by Rose Design

Church Publishing, Incorporated.
445 Fifth Avenue
New York, New York 10016

www.churchpublishing.com

Printed in the United States of America

CONTENTS

INTRODUCTION

The last three decades have seen a radical reorientation of the Episcopal Church around the centrality of baptism, wrought by the 1979 Book of Common Prayer. Two vignettes, just a few decades apart, may help illustrate the nature of the changes brought about by the introduction of the prayer book's baptismal rite.

I was baptized in the afternoon, with my parents, godparents, grandparents, and a very few friends of the family gathered around a small font in a side area of a large church that my immediate family did not attend regularly. It happened within seven months of my birth, and if there was any substantive prebaptismal preparation of my parents and godparents, it has been forgotten in the mists of time. In accordance with the prayer book of the day (this was the last gasp of the 1928 book), my baptism was a simple, brief matter to be dispensed with as rapidly as possible, and it was aimed primarily at washing off original sin and keeping me out of hell. My first communion, if it was thought of at all, would be expected to follow several years later, after I had been confirmed and "understood" the sacraments. This was a fairly typical baptism under the 1928 prayer book.

Almost thirty-six years later, at the Great Vigil of Easter, I took part in the baptism of two undergraduates at the university chapel where I am on staff. They had participated in the catechumenate over the prior eight months, gathering weekly to hear the story of God's action for God's people over the centuries and to share in small groups the story of their own lives. They met individually with sponsors as well. When they came to the font—a large font placed dead-center in the aisle, big enough to immerse an infant (as we would do at the Vigil in subsequent years)—it was the culmination of a long process of formation. The

CELEBRATING THE RITES OF INITIATION

undergrads promised before a congregation of several hundred to maintain the apostles' teaching and eucharistic fellowship, to seek and serve Christ in all persons, and to work for justice and peace. Next, they were drenched with water and then chrismated by the bishop as he imposed his hands on them. Finally, they received their first communion alongside the rest of the assembly.

The contrast between these two baptismal liturgies could not be greater. The 1928 baptismal rite was structured as a separate liturgy, although it could also take place after the second lesson in the daily office; the 1979 rite is structured as a ritual mass, taking place in the context of the eucharist. The 1928 book assumed that the normative candidate was an infant; the 1979 book assumes that the normative baptismal candidate is an adult.[1] The 1928 rite was focused on washing the candidate from sin, with relatively little emphasis on joining the body of Christ; the 1979 rite gives considerably more attention to baptism's function of bringing new members into the body of Christ. In the 1928 rite's vows, the candidate (or godparents) made minimal promises about living out the Christian faith, restricted to "Wilt thou then obediently keep God's holy will and commandments, and walk in the same all the days of thy life?"[2] while the 1979 rite's baptismal covenant involves extensive promises about behavior and action.[3] Finally, the 1928 rite assumed that baptism did not lead to the reception of communion, requiring confirmation first; by contrast, the 1979 rite expects that the newly baptized will proceed to communion without delay. The differences between the two liturgies are stark.

These ritual differences reflect deep differences in theology. In those places where the 1979 prayer book has been fully accepted and its theological and liturgical norms implemented, Episcopalians have come to see themselves as part of the body of Christ through their baptisms, commissioned with particular responsibilities to live the life of faith in the world. In those places, the reservation of baptism to four baptismal feasts (All Saints' Day, the Baptism of our Lord, the Day of Pentecost, and, above all others, the Great Vigil of Easter) promotes reflection on baptism in the light of the readings of the day and the thematic elements of the church calendar. Where the 1979 BCP and its teaching have been fully incorporated, our initiatory process and our common life are both the richer for it.

In the first chapter of this book, we will look at this distinctive ethos of the 1979 prayer book's baptismal liturgy. This necessarily entails a bit of history in addition to theology, which may at first glance seem out of place in a guide to the performance of the initiatory rites. But to understand why certain practices are recommended and others are not—and more importantly, to make responsible choices among the available options and to be able to adapt to one's context—practitioners must have some understanding of the ethos of the prayer book. That understanding requires some knowledge of the rites' evolution.

The 1979 prayer book decrees that baptism is "full initiation," but it also contains a rite for confirmation, reception, and reaffirmation, and it expects that individuals will undergo it. There are some internal contradictions around these rites, reflecting in part the history of the prayer book's development. The revision process came close to eliminating confirmation as a separate rite; the rite was preserved through a series of (largely political) events. Yet the 1979 baptismal rite itself includes bits that clearly were intended to reunite the pieces of the early church's initiation rite and eliminate the need for confirmation entirely. Further, if baptism truly is "full initiation," it is not immediately clear why anyone should be expected to be confirmed at all. The history of the 1979 prayer book's initiatory rites is ably mapped by Ruth Meyers, in her masterful *Continuing the Reformation*, and so there is no need to rehearse the same ground here.[4] But our discussion must come to grips with the internal contradictions in the 1979 book's initiatory rites as it sorts through the theology of confirmation and related rites.

As the 1979 prayer book was coming into being, the Roman Catholic Church and other churches in the West revived the ancient catechumenate as a means of preparing candidates for baptism. A version of this process was published in 1979 in the first edition of the *Book of Occasional Services*. Subsequently, in 1988, the Standing Liturgical Commission produced an adaptation of the catechumenate for those preparing for confirmation, reception, or the reaffirmation of baptismal vows. The lived experience in several places shows that the catechumenate, in all its fullness, offers an ideal process of preparation, whether for catechumens (those seeking baptism) or for those baptized persons intending to renew their vows in confirmation, reception, or reaffirmation. In chapter three, we will examine the catechumenal rites and discuss ways to bring this means of baptismal preparation to the local parish.

Good theology and good liturgical text do not guarantee good ritual practice. In too many cases, the prayer book's principles are undercut by bad performance. Sometimes this is the result of deliberate choice, sometimes of mere sloppiness, but the effects can be pernicious in either case. A colleague once shared the story of a rector who baptized monthly, without regard to the church calendar; omitted the baptismal covenant; did not instruct candidates, parents, or sponsors, or even rehearse the liturgy; and performed private baptisms on a frequent (nonemergency) basis. My colleague's experience of a conjunction of calendrical, textual, and catechetical sloppiness—a sort of *trifecta* of bad practice—is merely an extreme example of a common phenomenon. Bad initiatory practices are widespread, even if one rarely finds the sort of comedy of errors she encountered. Sometimes, prayer book principles are deliberately violated. Other times, the liturgy is marked by what can only be described as the careful, assiduous cultivation of the insipid, in what one might uncharitably think is a deliberate attempt to undercut what Christian initiation is supposed to be about. It is not uncommon to find, for example, baptisms in which the application of water is so sparing that it stands in wince-inducing contrast to the effusive imagery of Creation and the Red Sea contained in the Thanksgiving over the Water, the prayer uttered immediately prior to the action. I write this with firsthand knowledge, having grown up in a parish that used a two-ounce custard cup as the water container inside its brass baptismal bowl, to spare the altar guild from dealing with the mess of too much water.

Many of us have seen clergy and communities that managed to suck the life out of what is supposed to be the life-altering experience of initiation. No one would assume that they do this out of evil intent: far from it. But whether through ignorance or deliberate choice, the effect is to undercut the baptismal theology of the Church.[5] Good ritual practice matters, and so a large portion of the book will focus on advice on the performance of the liturgy.

This book is one in a series of ceremonial guides, which means that it need not revisit ground covered ably by others. Readers are well advised to consult the first section of Patrick Malloy's *Celebrating the Eucharist: A Practical Ceremonial*

Guide of Clergy and Other Liturgical Ministers (New York: Church Publishing, 2007) for its discussion of principles in liturgical decision-making, the spirit of the presider, and vesture and liturgical space.

Finally, there has been much recent debate concerning the proper progression between baptism and eucharist, between font and table. Persons of good will and considerable learning have argued that the Episcopal Church should practice what is colloquially termed "open table" communion, in which any and all persons, whether baptized or not, receive the eucharist. Other persons, likewise of profound learning and pastoral sensibility, argue for retaining the traditional sequence that requires baptism before communion. Yet an equally serious threat to good order in the church, I will argue, is the practice of withholding communion from the baptized—specifically from small children. We will consider the boundary lines that "fenced the table" in the past and the appropriate point of entry to the table now and in the future. Rather than being a tangential discussion in a book on initiatory practices, the question of the relationship between baptism and the eucharist lies close to the heart of the rhythms of the Christian life.

The debts amassed in the writing of a book are considerable and not easily repaid.

Bishop Paul Marshall's scholarly work, much of it in his prior career as a liturgics professor, has been a significant resource, but more than that, he has been my mentor since before he first ordained me to the presbyterate in 1996. I am deeply grateful to him.

I am indebted to the clergy and people of All Saints' Chapel at The University of the South in Sewanee, Tennessee, who have allowed me to serve as priest associate and to participate in the catechumenal program for several years. This has been a formative experience for me no less than for the catechumens and candidates for reaffirmation. I am especially grateful to the Rev. Thomas R. Ward Jr., who as university chaplain first invited me to take part and later entrusted the program to me on his retirement, and who later cotaught with me a course for parish clergy on the catechumenate. His successor as chaplain, the

Rev. Thomas E. Macfie Jr., has continued my involvement in the catechumenate. Both have given the gift of their wisdom and friendship.

Finally, my greatest debt is the one I am least able to repay: to my wife, Jennie, and to my son, Will, for their patient and unfailing support. Jennie's myriad forms of support included providing illustrations for the book. Will's support included reminding me of the religious perceptiveness of small children, as well as telling me when it was time to put the work aside and ride bikes together. This book is dedicated to them, but my gratitude runs far deeper than words can convey.

Notes

1. A "liturgical norm" is "the standard according to which a thing is done." Aidan Kavanagh, *The Shape of Baptism: The Rite of Christian Initiation* (Collegeville, MN: Liturgical Press, 1978), 108–9.

2. *The Book of Common Prayer and Administration of the Sacraments and Other Rites and Ceremonies of the Church* (New York: The Episcopal Church, 1928), 277–78.

3. *The Book of Common Prayer and Administration of the Sacraments and Other Rites and Ceremonies of the Church* (New York: The Episcopal Church, 1979) [henceforth, BCP 1979], 304–5.

4. Ruth A. Meyers, *Continuing the Reformation: Re-Visioning Baptism in the Episcopal Church* (New York: Church Publishing, 1997).

5. For a perceptive account of bad practices—and why they should be avoided—see Paul V. Marshall, "Trite Rite: Field Notes on the Trivialization of Christian Initiation," in *Leaps and Boundaries: The Prayer Book in the 21st Century*, ed. Paul V. Marshall and Lesley A. Northup (Harrisburg, PA: Morehouse Publishing, 1997), 71–80.

Chapter 1

THE ETHOS OF THE 1979 BOOK OF COMMON PRAYER

The baptismal rite in the 1979 Book of Common Prayer represented a radical departure from its predecessor rites. It has put in place a new theology of baptism, focused less on washing from sin and more on making disciples; a new ecclesiology, shaped around the baptized members, not around the clergy; and a new initiatory process, centered around a baptismal rite that is complete in and of itself. These shifts have been paralleled by changes in the ritual procedure itself. Baptisms, which in earlier years were private and frequent, have become significant public occasions in the life of the worshipping assembly. In this chapter, we will examine the baptismal rite of the 1979 BCP to uncover its theology and liturgical ethos.

To appreciate the ethos of the 1979 prayer book, as well the radical nature of its revision, we must begin with a look at the situation the revisers inherited. The 1928 book included a baptismal rite and a baptismal theology that stretched back to the sixteenth century, in the midst of the English Reformation's attempt to purge the church of traditional religion.

ANGLICAN BAPTISM BEFORE 1979

Prior to the revision process leading to the 1979 Book of Common Prayer, the baptismal rite in the Episcopal Church was essentially that of Thomas Cranmer's

1552 Book of Common Prayer. In an earlier revision, in 1549, Cranmer had translated the medieval rite from Latin into English and had added some text from Lutheran baptismal rites. But in 1552 he had stripped out such medieval ceremonies as exorcism, the blessing of the font, and anointing the candidate with oil; reordered some components of the 1549 rite (for example, shifting the sign of the cross from before the water bath to afterward); and added a post-baptismal prayer of thanksgiving, asking God to "regenerate this infant" and to "receive him for thy own child by adoption." Both of Cranmer's rites included a lengthy charge to the godparents to ensure that the child was brought up to know the creed, the Ten Commandments, and the Lord's Prayer, and to live a godly life. Additionally, the book supplied a similar form for baptism in private houses—and private baptism became increasingly prevalent in early modern England.[1]

Later English prayer books, in 1559, 1604, and 1662, left Cranmer's basic structure intact. The 1662 book made a few minor changes to the baptismal liturgy, but only two significant ones. The 1662 book added a petition to "sanctify this water to the mystical washing away of sin" to the prayer just prior to its administration, and added a vow to "obediently keep God's holy will and commandments, and walk in the same" to the end of the affirmation of the creed.[2] The former restored some of the sacramental emphasis lost in the 1552 revision when the blessing of the font was dropped, while the latter was a step toward acknowledging that the Christian life is about behavior as well as belief. The 1662 prayer book also added a separate rite for the baptism of adults, though its structure and most of its content were drawn from the more familiar liturgy for the public baptism of infants.[3]

Cranmer's prayer books retained the medieval rite of confirmation—but reinterpreted for a Protestant church. In the early church, there had been a variety of baptismal procedures, and by the fourth century, a post-baptismal anointing became increasingly accepted as a part of the rite.[4] The Roman pattern, in which one post-baptismal anointing was reserved to the bishop, became the root of confirmation, once presbyters were allowed to baptize. This episcopal ceremony, designed for children after baptism and termed "confirmation," was quite separate from baptism in most of the West by the eighth and ninth centuries.[5] Cranmer discarded the anointing, kept the hand-laying, and transposed confirmation to serve as a way for adolescents to mark the completion of catechizing.[6] Later, English Protestants would use this justification, sometimes adding, as Richard Baxter did, that it allowed those baptized as infants to claim the baptismal covenant for themselves.[7] Cranmer's prayer books therefore made baptism the first stage of a two-part initiatory process.

Cranmer's baptismal rite was marked by several features. It was a rite for infants: Cranmer expected children to be baptized within days of birth, and because of the Church of England's monopoly status, it was impossible for him to imagine an unbaptized adult who was also a subject of the monarch. It was also framed as a washing from sin: baptism's purpose was the individual's spiritual cleansing. Baptism was sacramental, and the liturgical text asserted that the candidate was regenerated by the rite, but anything resembling the blessing of water had been removed, along with anointing. Finally, baptism was not, in itself, complete: the newly baptized was to be instructed, and later, at adolescence, return for confirmation. Only confirmation conferred full membership in the church.

The English prayer books had, of course, come to North America in the colonial era. When the newly founded Episcopal Church adopted the 1789 Book of Common Prayer, it used the existing English baptismal rite as its starting point, cutting it down while leaving the theology, with its emphasis on cleansing from sin, untouched. The next prayer book revision, in 1892, did nothing to change this. It added some stage directions, and it slightly altered the provisions to shorten the service.[8] Both books made similar changes to the form of baptism in private houses and the form for the baptism of adults, cutting material but retaining the underlying theology.[9] The American church still used Cranmer's baptismal rite.

The next American prayer book, in 1928, did not make substantive changes. The 1928 BCP streamlined the many, separate rites for adults and children, and domestic and church-based baptism into a single liturgical form (while offering a set of directions to indicate which parts of the liturgy might be done at home and which at the church[10]). Nevertheless, the rite still assumed the baptism of infants as normative. This was reflected in several places, not least in the rubrics, which most often referred to children, often without accommodation for adult candidates (for example, in the rubric concerning the gender of godparents).[11] The 1928 revision also adjusted some familiar texts and rubrics. The most significant change altered the blessing of the font, which had been added in 1662. The new form was changed to resemble, structurally, the eucharistic prayer, in place of what had been a collect.[12] Despite the textual changes, the theology of the baptismal rite remained the same as it had been in Cranmer's prayer book. The rite was primarily focused on cleansing the candidate from sin, whether original (the flawed nature we inherit at birth) or actual (those things one has actually done). Baptism in the 1928 BCP was framed as what my liturgics professor once termed "celestial fire insurance," and it was very much geared toward keeping the baby (and it was almost always a baby) out of hell. The imagery and language in the rite that concerned joining the body of Christ was minimal, while the emphasis on washing off sin and on regeneration was heavy.

The performance of the rite under the 1928 book was fundamentally similar to what it had been under Cranmer. Baptism according to the 1928 BCP was generally a private affair. As Ruth Meyers has shown, for all that the prayer book rubrics indicated that baptism should be done publicly in the presence of a congregation, the prevailing practice was for it to be done privately. Indeed, some commentators went out of their way to rationalize the prevailing practice, acknowledging the rubric but creating a large array of exceptions or stretching the meaning of "public" baptism to cover baptisms done in the church building but outside the normal schedule of public worship.[13] Infant baptism was normative—adult baptism was rare. Massey Shepherd, in his commentary on the 1928 BCP, insisted that the rite should be done in public with a congregation present, but he also urged that it be done as soon as possible after birth: "we are commanded in Scripture to bring little children to Christ. (Many parents are unpardonably lax in fulfilling this duty and privilege.)"[14] As one would expect, given such an insistence on early baptism, there was little preparation of either parents or sponsors of infant candidates, but there was also apparently little preparation of adult candidates.[15]

The 1928 American Book of Common Prayer, much like its predecessors, offered a baptismal rite that in its theology was largely indistinguishable from that authored by Cranmer. Nevertheless, the 1928 book streamlined the liturgical texts, and it showed the stamp of a higher churchmanship, with a mandatory consignation and an elaborate blessing of the water. These textual shifts would be further developed in the next revision, even as the theology of baptism would undergo a revolutionary change.

The process of revision

The revision process that culminated in the 1979 Book of Common Prayer was itself a significant change from the process used in prior revisions. For the first time, there was extensive field testing of new liturgical texts. The Standing Liturgical Commission (SLC) proposed an amendment to the church's constitution to allow trial use of new liturgies; the amendment passed its first reading in the 1961 General Convention and was given final approval in 1964. Also in 1964, the General Convention instructed the Commission to prepare a plan for prayer book revision, which was approved in 1967. The SLC's plan created several drafting committees, each with their own section of the prayer book. Committees were chaired by SLC members and staffed by persons appointed by the Commission. The committees drew on 260 consultants who reviewed their work. The committees then incorporated the responses before forwarding their drafts to the SLC, which had final review before the texts were published as *Prayer Book Studies*. These *Prayer Book Studies* were available for trial use, and a network of diocesan liturgical commissions was formed to gather feedback from parish use, forwarding this on to the SLC.[16]

Once a full range of liturgical services had been drafted (in *Prayer Book Studies* 18 through 24), this material was authorized by General Convention for trial use as *Services for Trial Use* (known colloquially as the "Green Book," for its olive cover) in 1970. A revision of these services, plus new material, was approved by the next General Convention in 1973 and published as *Authorized Service* (the "Zebra Book," for its unsettling cover). Further revisions were made and circulated as the Draft Proposed Book of Common Prayer. With a few changes, this was approved by General Convention as the Proposed Book of Common Prayer in 1976. It was given its second reading and final approval in 1979, as the Book of Common Prayer.[17]

This lengthy and exhaustive process was quite unlike that used in earlier prayer book revisions. The reliance on trial use meant that the liturgical texts had been thoroughly "road-tested" before given their final form. The drafting committees included liturgiologists, parish clergy, at least one anthropologist, two literature professors, and a poet.[18] There was extensive and broad scholarly input as a result. Liturgical study in the twentieth century had become increasingly ecumenical, as scholars studied at some of the same institutions, gathered for meetings, and shared an interest in the same texts from the early church. The result was substantial, informal interchange among the churches. In addition to these informal influences, the Standing Liturgical Commission consulted with other denominations and with other, autonomous churches within Anglicanism during the revision process.[19] The result of this wide consultation was a prayer book unlike any of its predecessors.

The baptismal theology of the 1979 Book of Common Prayer

In order to celebrate the initiation rites of the 1979 Book of Common Prayer with integrity, one must grasp the essential features of the prayer book's baptismal theology. It is marked by a baptismal ecclesiology, an emphasis on baptism as the entry into discipleship, and an assertion that baptism is full initiation.

Baptism became the defining identity marker for Episcopalians, and the church placed a renewed emphasis on the importance of the ministry of the laity in the world.[20] Looking at the church more broadly, the same insight was dawning in other denominations, as such diverse theologians as Hans Küng, Karl Rahner, Robert Hovda, and Robert Farrar Capon defined the church not as the institution but as the "whole people of God," with distinctions between the ordained and the laity being simply a matter of different gifts and functions, given by God for the sake of the people as a whole.[21] In this view, the liturgy does not belong to the institutional church, or to the clergy; it is the common property of the whole people of God. Liturgy is a "public work"—something done for the good of the people. The clergy, and more specifically the bishops and their presbyters, are ordained as custodians of word and sacrament, and so they have a particular accountability to the assembly for what happens in the liturgy. But they do not own the liturgy.

Further, the liturgy as constituted by the 1979 BCP (and as visible in the early church too) requires the active participation of the whole people of God—the entire liturgical assembly. As Rahner and Küng noted in the larger context, the whole people of God is involved in the liturgical act. As Louis Weil put it, "the celebration of the liturgy is the shared activity of all the assembled people."[22] The laity are understood to have an active role in each and every one of the liturgical forms in the 1979 prayer book.

In promoting the place of the laity and ordering the life of the church around baptism, the prayer book was quite explicit about two things: one became a member of the church solely through baptism, with no other additional rite required; and there was no two-stage process of membership, with the baptized as junior members and the confirmed as full members. The prayer book is quite explicit: "Holy Baptism is full initiation by water and the Holy Spirit into Christ's Body the Church." The book adds, "The bond which God establishes in Baptism is indissoluble."[23] One becomes a full member in baptism, and one cannot lose that status by any means.

This was, of course, a stunning reversal of traditional Anglican thought. From the earliest days of the reformed Church of England, baptism was only the first stage of initiation. It made one a member of a sort—one was still barred from participation in much of church life. According to the prayer book, one could not receive communion until one was confirmed. Many dioceses also demanded confirmation of those who would be married or stand as godparents. Ultimately, this rubric was not enforced for communion, but instead one was required to know the catechism—a standard of learning was required, rather than the prayer book's insistence on completion of a ritual. When the prayer book's requirement was loosened in 1662, to require that one be confirmed or "ready and desirous of confirmation," the church hierarchy focused its attention on the clergy, enforcing requirements that they prepare and present candidates for confirmation. Only in the eighteenth and nineteenth centuries did confirmation become popular and frequent; it was then that confirmation became the *de facto* prerequisite for communion, a status it continued to hold into the twentieth century.[24] For Anglicans before the mid-twentieth century, then, baptism was never full initiation.

Because infant baptism was the statistical norm in the Anglican tradition, proposals to make baptism "full initiation" ran squarely into the problem of whether communion should be offered to small children. The common practice in the nineteenth and early twentieth centuries had been to withhold communion until confirmation, but, influenced by the Parish Communion movement, at least by the 1950s some clergy were administering communion to unconfirmed children as young as five.[25] Some of those involved in the revision of the prayer book were initially wary of making baptism the gate to communion, envisioning at least some sort of delay, perhaps to age six or eight. Others took a different view, arguing that baptism should admit one to communion, regardless of the age of the candidate.[26] Ultimately, the 1970 General Convention authorized the admission of children to communion before they were confirmed. By making baptism full initiation, the 1979 prayer book had to fight the assumptions the church had absorbed from this long tradition. The image of confirmation as an essential blessing and a completion of baptism was powerful in the imagination of some of Anglo-Catholic sympathies, while those of a more Evangelical persuasion insisted that one could not participate in a sacrament without knowledge and understanding of its meaning. A rubric in the proposed text for the baptismal rite would have required communion of the neophytes at their baptism, regardless of age, but this was dropped at some point between the 1975 revision of the text and the *Draft Proposed Book* of 1976.[27] Nevertheless, the articulation of baptism as "full initiation" implied admission to communion. Finally, in 1988, the House produced a set of guidelines for infant communion that affirmed communicating infants at their baptism, leaving subsequent communion until such time as the children and their parents ask for it.[28] The 1988 edition of the *Book of Occasional Services* included a rubric inviting (but not requiring) communion of the newly baptized infant; the initial draft would have mandated it.[29]

When to baptize

Prayer books before the 1979 Book of Common Prayer had restricted baptism to Sundays and holy days, but there was considerable departure from this, particularly in sixteenth- and seventeenth-century England. In actual practice, baptism generally took place in private, apart from the Sunday liturgy, and for the well-to-do, frequently in private houses.[30] In later centuries, clergy counted it as fitting to hold baptism only on Sundays or major feasts, but even these baptisms were generally not done as part of the public liturgy of the church: they happened afterward, with only family and friends present.[31] Baptism was seen as an individual affair, not a concern of the community, and there was little incentive to perform it in public. Further, the dangers of hellfire pressed toward administering baptism as soon as possible, so there would be strong disincentive to waiting for a public liturgy.

The 1979 prayer book changed this pattern by insisting that baptism be done at the principal liturgy of the day on a Sunday or major feast. No longer could one avoid doing baptism in public. In the baptismal ecclesiology of the 1979 BCP, the life of the people of God was ordered around baptism. Baptism, therefore, became public business.

Further, by baptizing in the midst of the principal liturgy of the day, the entire congregation was put in mind again of this foundational sacrament. They saw the action, they heard the readings and prayers, and, perhaps most importantly, they renewed their own baptismal covenant, reciting it along with the candidates. While good ritual never intends to be didactic, it can have the secondary effect of shaping our thinking, even our vocabulary. The repetition of the baptismal liturgy, and particularly the congregational recitation of the baptismal covenant, has helped to inculcate baptismal theology and baptismal ecclesiology in Episcopalians' consciousness—something that could never have been accomplished in the days of private baptism.

It was one thing to insist that baptism be done in public, but the 1979 prayer book went still further. It stipulated that baptisms really should be reserved to four calendrical occasions thematically linked to baptism, or to the bishop's visitation.[32] Of the calendrical days, three of them were traditionally associated with baptism (the Great Vigil of Easter, Pentecost, and the feast of the Baptism of our Lord). The Easter Vigil is perhaps the most ancient of baptismal occasions; in the early church, baptisms were often reserved to that one time each year. Pentecost, with its thematic imagery of the gift of the Spirit, and the Baptism of our Lord (observed in the East on Epiphany, not the Sunday following), with its story of Jesus' own baptism, also emerged quite early as baptismal occasions.[33] The other day on which baptisms are encouraged in the 1979 prayer book is All Saints' Day, which lent itself to baptism because it was a celebration of the communion of all the faithful, into which the newly baptized was being grafted. The bishop's visit was a logical occasion because the new prayer book makes the bishop the chief minister of baptism.

By restricting baptism to these days, the prayer book did several things. First, it ensured that the readings and other proper texts of the day would be in keeping with the ritual occasion, not least in helping to support the homiletical weight of a sermon on baptism and the baptismal life. Second, by limiting baptism to four or perhaps five occasions in the year, it ensured that in medium- and large-sized parishes, at least, there would be more than one candidate for initiation. This would help undermine the tendency to celebrate the individual, rather than the baptismal calling and baptismal life—something we will examine in a later chapter. Finally, by providing for four calendrical occasions that are spaced throughout the church year, and allowing for the recitation of the baptismal covenant in place of the Nicene Creed at the eucharist when there are no baptisms on those days, the prayer book has embedded baptism in the cycle of the Christian year as a regular part of Episcopalians' corporate life.

The restriction of baptism to certain occasions in the church year may not have excited as much opposition in the revision process as some other changes. Nevertheless, it is one of the most likely to be contested—or outright ignored—at the level of the local parish. We will take this up in a later chapter.

Whom to baptize

Earlier prayer books had assumed that the candidate for baptism was an infant. Indeed, there had been significant canonical legislation in the Middle Ages to ensure that children were baptized within days of their birth, and the early modern English prayer books had continued that inheritance. American prayer books dropped the insistence that candidates be baptized within eight days, but it was still expected that parents would promptly bring their infants to the font. While the 1662 English prayer book had added a form of baptism for "those of riper years," adult baptism was simply a corrective for the problem of persons born in the Interregnum, after the English Civil Wars of the seventeenth century, in which religious toleration had meant that some went unbaptized. With the return of the established church in 1660 and the prayer book in 1662, there was a backlog. The American prayer book had perpetuated that liturgical form through the 1892 revision, in 1928 merging it as a set of rubrics accompanying the form for the baptism of infants. But in no case was there any expectation that it would be used frequently.

In the 1979 revision, the Standing Liturgical Commission deliberately changed this. The new rite understood the baptism of adults as the "liturgical norm"—it was the sort of baptism that gave shape to the rite and from which the rite drew its meaning.[34] This shift was enacted in large and small ways. Adult candidates were presented first, before infants and younger children. Structural changes, such as the addition of the baptismal covenant, assumed that there were candidates who could make promises for themselves. Rubrics and directions, such as those suggesting that the newly baptized present the bread and wine at the offertory, presumed adult neophytes, and when a rubric described both adult and infant candidates, adults were listed first.[35]

This shift was due in part to the recognition of the changed culture in which the churches operated in the twentieth century. The "Christendom" model of the relationship between church on the one hand and the culture and state on the other, in place since Constantine first extended imperial favor to Christianity, had eroded. The norm of infant baptism had evolved in this context, but the context had changed. Increasing secularization in the West, beginning with the Enlightenment but accelerating in the twentieth century, meant that the culture no longer did the work of evangelism and catechesis that it had done in the era of "Christendom."[36] More and more persons were "unchurched"—lacking any religious affiliation. More and more baptismal candidates—if the church did its work of evangelism—would be adults.

How to baptize

The most dramatic changes in the new baptismal rite were structural: the 1979 liturgy was in this respect quite different from its predecessors. Chrismation and the imposition of hands were added to the rite alongside the signing with the cross. Further, baptism is set in the context of the eucharist, with the reasonable implication that the newly baptized will receive communion, completing the historic initiatory sequence of baptism/chrismation/first communion.[37] The structure breaks into five main units:

1. *Word Liturgy*
   Opening acclamation
   Opening sentences
   Collect
   Lessons
   Gospel
   Sermon

2. *Presentation and Examination of the Candidates*
   Presentation of baptismal candidates
   Renunciations and adhesions
   Presentation of other candidates (for confirmation/reception/reaffirmation)

3. *Baptismal Covenant*
   Recitation of covenant
   Prayers for the candidates
   Thanksgiving over the Water
   Consecration of chrism

4. *The Baptism*
   Water baptism
   Prayer
   Imposition of hands with consignation and chrismation

Welcome of the newly baptized

Peace

5. *Holy Eucharist*

A chief procedural change was the reintroduction of chrismation, along with an explicit imposition of hands, joined to the signing with the cross that had been a post-baptismal ceremony in Anglicanism since the 1552 prayer book. As mentioned above, the initiatory rites in the first few centuries of the Christian church had, in many places, come to include one or more anointings and the imposition of hands, in addition to a water bath.[38] Of particular interest is the pattern in Rome: there, the candidate received a preliminary anointing; three-fold immersion; vesting in a white garment; anointing on the crown of the head by a presbyter; hand-laying and a final, second anointing (with chrism) by the bishop; and then reception of the eucharist. This second anointing was associated with the infusion of the Holy Spirit,[39] and by the early Middle Ages the prayer at that anointing invoked the sevenfold gifts of the Spirit, as we see in this version from the Gelasian Sacramentary in the eighth century:

> Almighty God, Father of our Lord Jesus Christ, who has made your servants to be regenerated of water and the Holy Spirit and has given them remission of all their sins, Lord, send upon them your Holy Spirit the Paraclete, and give them the spirit of wisdom and understanding, the spirit of counsel and might, the spirit of knowledge and godliness, and fill them with the spirit of fear of God, in the Name of our Lord Jesus Christ with whom you live and reign ever God with the Holy Spirit, throughout all ages of ages. Amen.[40]

Gradually the Roman pattern asserted itself in the Western church, with the expectation that baptism and a presbyteral anointing would be followed by final chrismation by the bishop.[41]

As the church grew in Western Europe, though, it was no longer possible for a bishop to preside at each baptism. There were too many congregations and not enough bishops, particularly as a new emphasis was placed on the importance of infant baptism in an age of high infant mortality and increasing fear about the eternal fate of the unbaptized.[42] The imposition of hands and chrismation was reserved to bishops, and this episcopal monopoly resulted in a fractured rite of initiation, as early as the fifth century in some places, with a water bath administered by a presbyter, to be followed at some later point by chrismation and hand-laying by the bishop.[43] This remained the pattern through the Middle Ages.

Thomas Cranmer's first prayer book in 1549 offered a baptismal rite that preserved remnants of the medieval baptismal liturgy, including a post-baptismal anointing by the priest. Anointing disappeared in the 1552 and subsequent prayer books, replaced by a consignation that the 1549 book had used as a pre-baptismal ceremony.[44]

Twentieth-century liturgical scholarship had drawn attention to the original, unified rite of initiation in the early church, which included various ceremonies such as anointing and hand-laying in addition to the water bath in baptism. The framers of the new prayer book accepted the water bath alone as sufficient, but saw the fullness of the rite as including imposition of hands and chrismation.[45] Their first draft of the initiation rites, *Prayer Book Studies 18*, restored a single, unified rite of baptism with the imposition of hands and anointing, presided over by a presbyter. Their fundamental assumption was that the unified rite was both a restoration of early church practice and a pastorally appropriate response to modern needs.[46] The candidates for baptism, whether infant or adult, would be dipped in the water and then prayed over with a prayer drawn from the Gelasian sacramentary's prayer for the gifts of the Spirit:

> Heavenly Father, we thank you that by water and the Holy Spirit you have bestowed upon these your servants the forgiveness of sins, and have raised them to the new life of grace. Strengthen and confirm them, O Lord, with the riches of your Holy Spirit: an inquiring and discerning spirit, a spirit of purpose and perseverance, a spirit to know and to love you, and a spirit of joy and wonder in all your works.[47]

This prayer had been used in the Book of Common Prayer since 1549, but in the *confirmation* rite, not the baptismal rite.[48] After this post-baptismal prayer, the bishop or priest presiding then imposed a hand on the head of each candidate, making the sign of the cross, "using Chrism if desired," with the formula, "*Name*, you are sealed by the Holy Spirit." In a sense, a separate rite of confirmation was now superfluous, as its essentials—hand-laying and prayer for the gifts of the Spirit—were now restored to the baptismal rite, from which they had spun off in the Middle Ages.

This draft was blocked from coming into the new prayer book by opposition, and so the Standing Liturgical Commission produced successive drafts retaining baptism with the imposition of hands but adding back in the rite of confirmation. Ultimately, the Draft Proposed Book of Common Prayer included "Confirmation with Forms for Reception and for the Reaffirmation of Baptismal Vows," providing different formulae at the hand-laying for confirmation, reception, and reaffirmation.[49] That liturgical pattern was then used in the final version and stands in the present prayer book. Within the baptismal rite, a change was made in the sequence of actions by allowing a shift in the location of the consignation. A candidate was immersed in the water bath, and then the presider had a choice: she could continue with the prayer for the gifts of the spirit, then the imposition of hands, sign of the cross, and optional anointing, or the celebrant could alter the sequence to water bath, imposition of hands with cross and optional chrism, and finally the prayer for the gifts of the Spirit. The same option was retained in the final version of the prayer book.[50] This was largely a concession to complaints from bishops about the practicality of separating the two actions of bath and imposition of hands/chrismation, while members of the Commission had tried to safeguard the two-stage structure of the liturgy by keeping the actions apart.[51]

By reuniting water-baptism with the imposition of hands (and consignation), and allowing for the optional use of chrism, the framers of the 1979 prayer book had managed to restore the primitive church's liturgy of initiation. The historic, pre-Reformation definition of confirmation had framed it as the imposition of hands and/or chrismation by the bishop subsequent to baptism, a view held by many modern scholars.[52] In this interpretation, baptism and confirmation were reunited in one liturgy. The persistence of a different view, traceable to the Reformation and holding that confirmation was not about anointing and hand-laying at all, but was really a mature, public affirmation of faith, taking place after (infant) baptism, accounts for the survival of a separate rite of "confirmation" in the prayer book.[53] But this survival should not obscure the achievement of the Standing Liturgical Commission in including the imposition of hands and chrismation in the baptismal rite.

The eucharistic setting of the rite is also important. First, as noted above, the implicit expectation is that the neophytes will receive communion at their own baptisms. Because baptism is full initiation, there is no barrier to this, and it completes the ancient sequence of baptism/hand-laying/first communion. Second, the eucharistic context of one's baptism frames subsequent eucharistic participation as a renewal of that baptism. As Leonel Mitchell put it, "it is through baptism that the mighty saving acts of Christ become available to us. . . . Then the eucharist is the sacramental proclamation and celebration of that covenant relationship."[54] The eucharist nurtures and sustains the relationship that was created in baptism. In a sense, each time one comes to the table, one repeats the third, repeatable part of Christian initiation.

BAPTISMAL COVENANT

As well as adding chrismation and the eucharistic setting, the drafters of the 1979 prayer book added a new structural unit, the baptismal covenant. The covenant, which is separate from the renunciations and adhesions common to many baptismal rites, has proved to be one of the most significant changes in the baptismal rite, setting the 1979 BCP apart from its predecessors and from parallel worship books in other, contemporary Anglican bodies.

The covenant begins with an interrogatory form of the Apostles' Creed, the historic baptismal creed. Quite powerfully, the whole assembly joins in the recitation along with the candidates, as well as in the questions that follow. The recitation of the creed in itself was something of a departure from previous American rites, which asked if one believed the articles of the Apostles' Creed without reciting them, and from previous English prayer books, in which the minister recited the creed but the candidates and sponsors did not.[55] In the 1979 BCP, the minister prompts the candidates with questions ("Do you believe in God the Father?"), to which they reply with the creed, paragraph by paragraph ("I believe in God, the Father almighty, creator of heaven and earth . . .").

After this, the presider asks the candidates questions that work out the implications of Christian faith in one's daily life. The first question asks if they will participate in the sacramental life of the church: "Will you continue in the apostles' teaching and fellowship, in the breaking of bread, and in the prayers?" This makes the important point that Christian faith is lived corporately, as a part of the liturgical assembly. There is no such thing as "private" religion, in the life of the baptized: we exist as part of a worshipping body. The next question asks if the candidates will persist in resisting evil and repent when they sin. Here, the prayer book takes a remarkably realistic view of human capacity: the question is not *if* they will sin, but what they will do *when* they sin. Another question asks the candidates if they will proclaim the gospel in word and action.[56] This underscores the duty of the baptized to tell what they have seen and heard, and it also makes the point that actions tend to speak louder than words.

Finally, two questions squarely address the social implications of baptism. The first question asks, "Will you seek and serve Christ in all persons, loving your neighbor as yourself?" The second asks, "Will you strive for justice and peace among all people, and respect the dignity of every human being?"[57] The first demands equitable treatment of the others one encounters in one's life. The second points toward the need for Christians to combat systemic injustice, and it underscores that the love of neighbor is not restricted to other members of the Christian household: one is to respect the dignity of *every* human being, and the imperative is not dependent on discerning the Christ in the other person, as it was in the prior question.

The inclusion of the baptismal covenant emphasizes that baptism in the 1979 Book of Common Prayer is primarily about discipleship. It entails the taking on of serious obligations for Christian practice. It is not a charming ceremony done to an infant, nor is it simply the cleansing from sin. Throughout the rite, the theme of discipleship is emphasized. In the welcoming of the baptized, the assembly invited the neophytes to "confess the faith of Christ crucified, proclaim his resurrection, and share with us in his eternal priesthood."[58]

The theology of the prayer book liturgy is clear in the liturgical text, but for it to communicate its meaning, it must be effectively performed. We will turn to best practices in performance in a later chapter, but first we will look at the issues around confirmation.

Notes

1. F. E. Brightman, *The English Rite: Being a Synopsis of the Sources and Revisions of the Book of Common Prayer* (London: Rivingtons, 1915), 724–47.

2. Brightman, *English Rite*, 724–47. The spelling in all quotations has been modernized; the original spelling of all book titles has been retained.

3. Paul V. Marshall, *Prayer Book Parallels: The Public Services of the Church Arranged for Comparative Study*, vol. 1 (New York: Church Publishing, 1989), 284–304.

4. Maxwell E. Johnson, *The Rites of Christian Initiation: Their Evolution and Interpretation*, rev. ed. (Collegeville, MN: Liturgical Press, 2007), 203, 42, 61–67, 108.

5. Gerard Austin, *The Rite of Confirmation: Anointing with the Spirit* (New York: Pueblo Publishing, 1985), 18; J. D .C. Fisher, *Christian Initiation: Baptism in the Medieval West: A Study in the Disintegration of the Primitive Rite of Initiation* (London: Hillenbrand Books, 1965), 74–78, 89–95.

6. Thomas Cranmer, *Miscellaneous Writings and Letters of Thomas Cranmer*, ed. John Edmund Cox for the Parker Society (Cambridge, UK: Regent College Publishing, 1846), 80; British Library Cotton MS Cleo E.v, fol. 73–101; Bryan Spinks, "Cranmer, Baptism, and Christian Nurture; or, Toronto Revisited," *Studia Liturgica* 32 (2002), 105.

7. Richard Baxter, "To the Christian Reader," in Jonathan Hanmer, *Teleiosis: Or, an Exercitation upon Confirmation, The Ancient Way of Completeing Church-Members* (London: by A. Maxey for John Rothwell, 1657), n.p.

8. Marshall, *Prayer Book Parallels*, 234, 240–56, 266–80, 300–308.

9. Marshall, *Prayer Book Parallels*, 266–80.

10. Marshall, *Prayer Book Parallels*, 266–79.

11. Marshall, *Prayer Book Parallels*, 232–38.

12. Marshall, *Prayer Book Parallels*, 254–55.

13. Meyers, *Continuing the Reformation*, 7–8.

14. Massey Hamilton Shepherd Jr., *The Oxford American Prayer Book Commentary* (New York: Oxford University Press, 1950), 273.

15. Meyers, *Continuing the Reformation*, 9–10.

16. Meyers, *Continuing the Reformation*, 125–27; Jeffrey Lee, *Opening the Prayer Book*, The New Church's Teaching Series, vol. 7 (Cambridge, MA: Cowley Publications, 1999), 81–82.

17. Meyers, *Continuing the Reformation*, 127–28.

18. *Journal of the General Convention of the Protestant Episcopal Church in the United States of America* (New York: The Episcopal Church, 1970), 518–20; *Journal of the General Convention of the Protestant Episcopal Church in the United States of America* (New York: The Episcopal Church, 1976), AA288–91.

19. Marion J. Hatchett, *Commentary on the American Prayer Book* (New York: Seabury Press, 1981), 13.

20. Louis Weil, *A Theology of Worship* (Cambridge, MA: Cowley Publications, 2002), 11–14, 20; Leonel L. Mitchell, *Praying Shapes Believing: A Theological Commentary on the Book of Common Prayer* (Harrisburg, PA: Morehouse Publishing, 1985), 294.

21. Karl Rahner, *The Church and the Sacraments*, trans. W. J. O'Hara (London: Burns & Oates, 1963, 1974), 11–19; Hans Küng, *The Church*, trans. Ray Ockenden and Rosalenn Ockenden (London: Burns & Oates, 1967), 125–26, 184–87, 205–10, 395, 422, 427, 438–39; Robert W. Hovda, *Strong, Loving, and Wise: Presiding in Liturgy* (Collegeville, MN: Liturgical Press, 1976), 2–7; Robert Farrar Capon, "The Ordination of Women: A Non-Book," *Anglican Theological Review*, Supplementary Series 2 (1973): 71.

22. Weil, *Theology of Worship*, 7.

23. BCP 1979, 298.

24. James F. Turrell, "Confirmation, Conversion, and Catechizing: Patterns of Incorporation in the Early Modern Church of England" (PhD diss., Vanderbilt University, 2002).

25. David R. Holeton, "Communion of All the Baptized and Anglican Tradition" *Anglican Theological Review* 69 (1987): 25.

26. Meyers, *Continuing the Reformation*, 134–35.

27. Leonel Mitchell, "The Communion of Infants and Little Children," *Anglican Theological Review* 71 (1989): 76.

28. Meyers, *Continuing the Reformation*, 235.

29. Mitchell, "Communion of Infants and Little Children," 76.

30. David Cressy, *Birth, Marriage, and Death: Ritual, Religion, and the Life-Cycle in Tudor and Stuart England* (Oxford, UK: Oxford University Press, 1997), 188–94.

31. Meyers, *Continuing the Reformation*, 7–8, 48–52.

32. BCP 1979, 312.

33. Hatchett, *Commentary*, 255–56; Thomas J. Talley, *The Origins of the Liturgical Year*, 2nd ed. (Collegeville, MN: Liturgical Press, 1991), 33–37, 121–29; but cf. Paul F. Bradshaw and Maxwell E. Johnson, *The Origins of Feasts, Fasts, and Seasons in Early Christianity* (Collegeville, MN: Liturgical Press, 2011), 75–86, 146–47.

34. See the helpful definition of a "liturgical norm" in Kavanagh, *Shape of Baptism*, 108.

35. BCP 1979, 301, 302, 304–5, 313.

36. Kavanagh, *Shape of Baptism*, 154–55.

37. Mitchell, *Praying Shapes Believing*, 116–17.

38. Johnson, *Rites of Christian Initiation*, 203, 42, 61–67, 108. Note that instead of locating the origins of confirmation in this post-baptismal anointing and imposition of hands

for the conferral of the Holy Spirit, as most liturgiologists argue, Aidan Kavanagh views the imposition of hands as merely an elaborate dismissal of the newly baptized from their baptismal ritual into their first eucharist. Consequently, confirmation had nothing to do with the bestowal of the Spirit, and "confirmation should not be made too much over." Aidan Kavanagh, *Confirmation: Origins and Reform* (New York: Pueblo Books, 1988), 117 and passim.

39. Paul F. Bradshaw, Maxwell E. Johnson, and L. Edward Phillips, *The Apostolic Tradition: A Commentary* (Minneapolis, MN: Fortress Press, 2002), 112–35; Johnson, *Rites of Christian Initiation*, 134; Kavanagh, *Shape of Baptism*, 50–63.

40. E. C. Whitaker and Maxwell E. Johnson, *Documents of the Baptismal Liturgy* (Collegeville, MN: Liturgical Press, 2003), 235.

41. Leonel L. Mitchell, *Baptismal Anointing* (London: S.P.C.K., 1966), 125; Leonel L. Mitchell, *Worship: Initiation and the Churches* (Washington, DC: Pastoral Press, 1991), 199–200; Austin, *Rite of Confirmation*, 17–18; Marion J. Hatchett, "The Rite of 'Confirmation' in The Book of Common Prayer and Authorized Services 1973," *Anglican Theological Review* 55 (1974): 294–95. For two notable exceptions in the Ambrosian rite and the Mozarabic rite, see Mitchell, *Worship*, 75–102.

42. Johnson, *Rites of Christian Initiation*, 203; Austin, *Rite of Confirmation*, 14–16.

43. Austin, *Rite of Confirmation*, 14–15.

44. Brightman, *English Rite*, 740–43, 728.

45. See Leonel L. Mitchell, "The Theology of Christian Initiation and the *Proposed Book of Common Prayer*," *Anglican Theological Review* 60 (1978): 408–10; Leonel L. Mitchell, "Place of Baptismal Anointing," *Anglican Theological Review* 68 (1986): 205–8.

46. Standing Liturgical Commission, *Holy Baptism with the Laying-on-of-Hands: Prayer Book Studies 18* (New York: Church Hymnal Corporation, 1970) [henceforth, *PBS 18*], 19–22.

47. *PBS 18*, 39.

48. Brightman, *English Rite*, 794–95; Marshall, *Prayer Book Parallels*, 432–33.

49. Draft Proposed Book of Common Prayer (New York: Church Hymnal Corporation, 1976), 414–21.

50. Draft Proposed BCP, 309–10; BCP 1979, 307–8.

51. Meyers, *Continuing the Reformation*, 181, 184.

52. Daniel Stevick, *Baptismal Moments, Baptismal Meanings* (New York: Church Hymnal Corporation, 1987), 15–17, 55; J. D. C. Fisher, "History and Theology," in *Confirmation Crisis* (New York: Seabury Press, 1968), 29, 38, 41–42; Leonel L. Mitchell, "Christian Initiation, Rites of Passage, and Confirmation," in *Confirmation Re-Examined* ed. Kendig Brubaker Cully (Wilton, CT: Morehouse-Barlow, 1982), 90–91.

53. Stevick, *Baptismal Moments*, 21–23, 55; Mitchell, "Christian Initiation," 88–89.

54. Leonel L. Mitchell, "Should the Unbaptized Be Welcomed to the Lord's Table?" *Open* (Fall 1994): 5–6.

55. Marshall, *Prayer Book Parallels*, 248–49; Brightman, *English Rite*, 736–37.

56. BCP 1979, 304

57. BCP 1979, 305.

58. BCP 1979, 308.

Chapter 2

MAKING SENSE OF CONFIRMATION, RECEPTION, AND REAFFIRMATION OF BAPTISMAL VOWS

The 1979 Book of Common Prayer describes baptism as "full initiation," demoting the rite of confirmation from its previous status as the completion of the initiatory process. As we have discussed, the revisers of the Book of Common Prayer tried initially to eliminate confirmation entirely (in *Prayer Book Studies 18*), then created a repeatable rite of reaffirmation (in *Prayer Book Studies 26*), before allowing a nonrepeatable confirmation rite to return by inches, due largely to pressure from the bishops of the church.[1] But the rite of confirmation in the 1979 BCP does not carry the same freight as the historical rite. For those who focused on the classical definition of confirmation as anointing and imposition of hands for the gift of the Holy Spirit, identified with the Catholic wing of the church, the restoration of post-baptismal anointing in the 1979 baptismal rite made confirmation irrelevant. For those who focused on the Reformation definition of confirmation as a sort of graduation ceremony after catechizing, a position identified more frequently with the Evangelical wing of the church, the admission of children to communion apart from confirmation devalued the significance of that "graduation." No longer truly initiatory, and bearing neither a unique gift of the Spirit nor a meal ticket for communion, confirmation has changed. It is now a "pastoral rite" that publicly marks the mature affirmation of faith made in the presence of the bishop.

Because confirmation is still with us, parish clergy and bishops must make the best of a muddled situation. The key issues in the use of the current rite are first, the intended purpose of the rite (what is the rite trying to do); second, the appropriate subject of the rite (who should undergo it); and third, the performance of the rite (how the rite should be done).

CONFIRMATION'S PURPOSE

As a pastoral rite, confirmation's scope is more limited in the 1979 book than it ever has been since the days of the early church, when it was the modest dismissal described by Aidan Kavanagh.[2] Confirmation now is a public commitment to baptismal promises, made in the presence of the bishop, after which the person making the promises receives the bishop's blessing, signified by the imposition of hands. Its importance is strictly derivative of baptism—the sacrament in which the promises were originally made.

Confirmation is now joined to two cognate rites, reception and the reaffirmation of baptismal vows. The liturgical form for reception offers a way to ritualize a person's entry into the communion of the Episcopal Church from some other denomination. The form for reaffirmation of baptismal vows allows a person to make a public recommitment to baptismal promises, in the presence of the bishop. Liturgically, the two forms are virtually the same as confirmation: the only difference is in the formula said over the candidate and the omission of a rubric requiring an accompanying hand-laying at reception and reaffirmation, in contrast to confirmation.

This similarity provides further clues about the prayer book's view of confirmation. The rite of reception involves a conscious decision to leave one ecclesial community and enter another. It is about choice and embrace: an act of assent. The rite of reaffirmation of baptismal vows is an act of commitment, renewing vows once made. It, too, is an act of assent. Linking confirmation to reception and reaffirmation highlights the sixteenth-century interpretation of confirmation as an act of commitment, of "owning the covenant."

Confirmation, reception, and reaffirmation are structurally identical, and the only clear differences in theological content are found in the distinctive formulae at the imposition of hands. In confirmation, the presider asks God to "Strengthen, O Lord, your servant N. with your Holy Spirit; empower *him* for your service; and sustain *him* all the days of *his* life," or to "Defend, O Lord, your servant N. with your heavenly grace, that *he* may continue yours for ever, and daily increase in your Holy Spirit more and more, until *he* comes to your everlasting kingdom. *Amen.*" God is asked to strengthen or defend the individual, not to provide something previously lacking. The formula for reception is still more limited in its scope: "N., we recognize you as a member of the one holy catholic and apostolic Church, and we receive you into the fellowship of this Communion. God, the Father, Son, and Holy Spirit, bless, preserve, and keep you." God is asked to bless the candidate in a generic sort of way, without any particular effect requested; indeed, most of the formula is addressed to the candidate, not the Almighty, in contrast to the confirmation formulae. Finally, the formula at the reaffirmation of baptismal vows is equally restrained: "N., may the Holy Spirit, who has begun a good work in you, direct and uphold you in the service of Christ and his kingdom." The formula is addressed to the candidate, not God, with the subjunctive wish that the Spirit might continue to guide the candidate.[3] There are differences among the formulae, but all of them are quite modest in their requests of the Almighty.

The focus of the rite remains on the promises made by the candidate, which are simply a recommitment to the vows made in baptism. The candidates reaffirm their renunciation of evil and renew their commitment to Jesus Christ, and then they and the entire congregation join in the recitation of the baptismal covenant. No further promises are made.

Neither confirmation nor reaffirmation, therefore, are rites of membership. Reaffirmation is, of course, intended for those who have previously been confirmed, so it is unsurprising that it does not have this function. But confirmation has sometimes been erroneously construed as conveying denominational membership: one is baptized into generic Christianity, but one is confirmed into Episcopal identity.[4] The language of the rite itself suggests nothing of the sort, and the history of the rite, as a minor portion of the baptismal liturgy, further undercuts this claim.

Even the rite of reception does not explicitly involve promises by the candidate to adhere to the Episcopal Church. The formula said by the bishop states simply, "We recognize you as a member of the one holy catholic and apostolic Church," which does not connote specific denominational loyalty, and "we receive you into the fellowship of this Communion," which is fairly restrained. Reception functions to mark a change in identity, but the rite's own content barely acknowledges this role.

If confirmation is not about denominational identity, still less is it an act of fealty to the bishop. Nor, for that matter, is it about creating some sort of pastoral relationship between the bishop and the confirmand, although some have claimed exactly that.[5] Similar claims, that confirmation can maintain unity in a diocese or combat insidious congregationalism within the Episcopal Church, simply cannot be supported by evidence.[6] Confirmation, to the degree that it is relational, is about the relationship between the candidate, who is renewing baptismal promises, and the Lord into whom she was baptized. The bishop's function, at most, is as symbolic representative of the larger church, witnessing this renewal and offering her (modest) blessing.[7]

For that matter, confirmation itself, as currently constructed, is not about education *per se*. The rite's directions make reference to preparation as a prerequisite, but ask only that the candidate be "duly prepared," without specifying the nature of that preparation. Again, the heart of confirmation is the renewal of baptismal promises, made in the presence of the bishop, who supplies her blessing through the imposition of hands.

As a result, attempts to reinvent (or recover) confirmation as a means of ensuring adequate Christian education quickly run aground. It is not for want of trying: many recent writers have paired confirmation and catechizing, and well-meaning clergy sometimes conflate confirmation with the classes that conventionally prepare persons for the rite. Several of the essays produced by the Theology Committee of the House of Bishops of the Episcopal Church in 2005 made this link between catechetical formation and confirmation, justifying the rite in terms of the instruction that precedes it, and devising requirements (including a standardized curriculum and regular testing) both exhaustive and exhausting.[8] Anglican cultural memory bears the marks of the sixteenth and seventeenth centuries, when confirmation was reinvented as a graduation ceremony after catechizing. Yet the current rite is something else.

Finally, confirmation is not the completion of baptism. One bishop has claimed that bishops have an "essential" role in "sealing" the newly baptized, an argument that was historically myopic, but also ignored the very words of the prayer book itself.[9] After all, the "sealing" of baptism is now done in the baptismal rite, when the celebrant says to the newly baptized, "N., you are sealed by the Holy Spirit in Baptism and marked as Christ's own for ever."[10] One theologian has argued that confirmation somehow activates the Christian's faith and practice: "[W]hat is already made real for us at baptism—our becoming one with Christ (Christ's own) and therefore set upon a new way of living—begins to be manifested as our own activity for a whole new way of life at confirmation."[11] But this ignores the baptismal covenant, the practice of adult baptism, and the realities of developmental psychology. In the covenant, the candidate for baptism promises that the new way of life begins at once.[12] Adult candidates for baptism have already begun to manifest their commitment to Christ, which is why both Roman Catholics and Episcopalians quite explicitly include such candidates in the household of faith.[13] Even those baptized as infants live the baptismal covenant before confirmation, because very young children are developmentally capable of showing evidence of both faith and moral behavior, and of participating in the worship of the church. Confirmation completes nothing.

The quite forthright assertions of the prayer book that baptism is full initiation negate all attempts to carve out a bigger role for confirmation. It remains, at its core, the renewal of baptismal promises, a secondary rite. Baptism is primary, full, and complete in itself.

CONFIRMATION'S CANDIDATES (AND THOSE FOR RECEPTION AND REAFFIRMATION)

The post-baptismal anointing of the early church that broke free from the baptismal rite in the Middle Ages and was transformed into an adolescent rite of passage in the Reformation has become something else entirely: "[A] mature public affirmation of their faith and commitment to the responsibilities of their Baptism."[14]

The cognate rites of reception and reaffirmation of baptismal vows, which now stand alongside confirmation, are identically structured rites for a public statement of faith in the presence of the bishop. It follows, therefore, that the candidates for these rites, like confirmation candidates, must be "mature." The difficulty, of course, lies in how one assesses "maturity," a term that should be distinguished from "age-appropriate." To be mature is to be "complete in natural development or growth" and "having or expressing the mental and emotional qualities that are considered normal to an adult socially adjusted human being."[15] Thus, for an affirmation of faith to be "mature," it must be made by one who possesses the intellectual capacity, moral reasoning, and will of an adult. This requirement stands in marked contrast to the preconditions for baptism (in the case of infants) or reception of communion by those who have been baptized. One may disagree with the requirement that candidates be "mature," but one cannot ignore or dismiss it, for all that it may pose pastoral challenges.

Historically, the age of confirmation has fluctuated considerably, with infants as the normative candidates in the Middle Ages and youth as the candidates in the Reformation era. In some Episcopal parishes in the mid- to late-twentieth century, it was not uncommon to confirm persons as young as eight years old, with nine to twelve being the norm, perhaps reflecting Roman Catholic patterns, which set confirmation at the age of discretion (seven years). But such a borrowing would ignore the very different nature of Roman Catholic confirmation, which is not based on a mature affirmation of faith. A paper published by the Theology Committee of the House of Bishops in 2005, describing "best practices," argued that it should be delayed to "a minimum age of confirmation of 15 years."[16] Yet even this minimum is not necessarily the most appropriate age for a "mature" affirmation.

Urban Holmes argued decades ago that confirmation took place at too young an age. He protested against the practice of confirming nine- to twelve-year-olds, but his argument was that the "age of maturity" fell much later: "I would suggest that it falls between the ages of 18 and 25, and I would emphasize the later end of the spectrum."[17] While it is a truism among parents and outside observers that individuals weather considerable changes in early adolescence, psychologists have provided a more nuanced view of the dynamics at work. Research suggests that "personality traits become increasingly stable over the life span," with stability significantly increasing in late adolescence and early adulthood:

> The transition to adolescence is perhaps the most volatile normative transition in the life span, entailing a coalescence of social, cognitive, and biological changes. It is associated with rapid maturational changes, shifting societal demands, exploration of new identities and roles, and the initiation of new peer and romantic relationships. . . . [A]s individuals make the transition into adulthood, maturational changes are reduced, environmental changes are increasingly subject to individual control, and a more stable sense of self is formed.[18]

But personality is not the only aspect of the adolescent's changing mental world. The very capacity for thought is changing, and these changes, more than any other, have an impact on the individual's ability to make a mature affirmation of faith.

At an earlier age, the adolescent has barely achieved the capacity for abstract, conceptual thought, and the crucial task of identity formation has only begun. Indeed, according to several different developmental models, the thirteen- to seventeen-year-old is unlikely to be capable of the sort of mature affirmation that the prayer book defines confirmation to be. According to Erikson, adolescents are, until age eighteen, involved in the task of identity formation, experimenting with different roles and value systems. Researchers following Erickson's approach have found that it is during college years that increasing identity commitments are made. According to Piaget, formal operational thought (the capacity for thinking about abstract concepts) begins to appear in some children between twelve and fourteen. But in one large study, only thirty percent of thirteen-year-olds displayed formal thought, while sixty percent of college students did. This would tend to argue against confirmation in early adolescence, as does research by Lawrence Kohlberg on moral development in children. Kohlberg and others have found that the capacity to reason through a moral dilemma grows over time, with the most sophisticated moral reasoning not emerging until adolescence or the twenties.[19] If the affirmation of faith has any moral component—if "walking the walk" is taken as a part or a measure of "talking the talk"—a mature affirmation may not be possible until the end of adolescence.

James Fowler has built on these theorists' work to argue that there are stages in faith development, with a loose association between progression in stages and increase in age. Elementary-school children, for example, are likely to exhibit what Fowler terms "mythic-literal faith" in his second stage, although he notes that adolescents and adults can also stay at that stage of faith, and some individuals come to rest in the third stage of "synthetic-conventional faith," which emerges in adolescence, and in which one's faith is largely unexamined and is based on the authority of others. The next stage, "individuative-reflective" faith, emerges in late adolescence or early adulthood, and it is this stage of faith that can be described as "mature," as the individual takes responsibility for his or her own commitments. Only a few individuals will progress to the fifth and sixth stages of faith in Fowler's schema, of "conjunctive" and "universalizing" faith, in which one achieves a "second naiveté" (borrowing from Ricoeur) and embraces a multifaceted view of truth, in stage five, before some few in stage six achieve a radically self-giving faith.[20]

No single developmental model should be seen as decisive, and individuals do not move through a model in lockstep according to a set schedule.[21] One would therefore want to be careful about setting too high a bar for confirmation candidates in general, and one would also want to be open to the possibility that one might encounter individuals who achieve "maturity" far ahead of their peers. For that matter, there will always be pastoral exceptions to be made for those who are cognitively or developmentally challenged; what is of concern here is the normative pattern. But developmental models suggest that delaying confirmation to late adolescence at the earliest would increase the chance that persons would be able to make a mature affirmation of faith.

The practice in some parishes of substituting the "Rite 13" program for confirmation at its former age and then using confirmation to mark the completion of two years of the "Journey to Adulthood" curriculum, while very well intentioned, still falls victim to the constraints of human intellectual development. The shift does have the benefit of moving confirmation later, but the adolescent at age sixteen or seventeen is not substantially more able to make a truly mature affirmation of faith. By using the term "mature," the prayer book arguably fore-closes adolescent confirmation, whether the General Conventions of 1976 and 1979 intended this or not. At the very least, one must admit that a general prac-tice of confirming those under the age of eighteen substantially undermines the prayer book principle that confirmation is a "mature" affirmation of faith.

Candidates for confirmation therefore must be mature, and likely should be eighteen years of age at the very least, to keep within the confines of the prayer book's rubrics and directions. But implicit in the directions is also the expecta-tion that the candidates will have some basis for their affirmation. Obviously, they must be baptized, but more than that, they need to have some concept of the Christian faith and life, if they are now making a willful affirmation of that faith and life.

Candidates must therefore have received appropriate preparation for the promises that they will make. While the educational program that some have tried to attach to confirmation is more than the rite can carry, it is true that the prayer book and canons expect that candidates will be "duly prepared."[22] Indeed, because the rite is, at root, a reaffirmation of baptismal vows, it is important that candidates be prepared to affirm them with a reasonably full knowledge of the implications. This requires catechesis. But any catechesis that is to be done should locate confirmation in its baptismal context. In essence, the task is for candidates to give "informed consent" to the baptismal cov-enant. This is quite different than the typical "confirmation class," and even different from the proposed curriculum offered by the Theology Committee, all of which tend to make confirmation preparation a matter of learning Epis-copal lore, rather than being formed in Christian life. Christianity is a practice, not a body of knowledge to be mastered. Confirmation preparation, therefore, is not a sort of educational exercise in the usual sense, nor should Christian formation be so tied to it that it becomes a one-time exercise, a hurdle to clear on the way to the bishop's imposition of hands. A later chapter will examine preparation in detail.

These preconditions of age and preparation set something of a high bar for candidates. The rationale for such a standard is the insistence of the prayer book (and the General Convention in the early 1970s, particularly the House of Bishops) that confirmation is a mature commitment. It would be wrong to apply anything remotely approximating such a standard to children as a precondition to eucharistic participation, just as no one would apply such a test to infant baptismal candidates. Indeed, quite small children are capable of living out the baptismal covenant, in all its aspects of faith, participation in worship, and moral action. The work of Sofia Cavalletti and others shows that children are able to express religious ideas and to participate in worship from a very early age.[23] There is considerable evidence that young children develop moral capacity in the preschool years. Young children begin to show evidence of distinguishing good and bad before age two, and they develop a sense of guilt at a similarly early age.[24] Very small children are fully capable of living the Christian life, in an age-appropriate way.

But the prayer book—and really, the determination of the bishops and General Convention in the early 1970s to retain confirmation and to imbue it with the meaning of a "mature affirmation"—has significantly constrained how we may approach confirmation and the preparation of candidates. If we are to keep in the spirit of the Book of Common Prayer, we cannot speak of "age-appropriate" affirmations of faith in connection with confirmation, because the BCP has determined that such an affirmation must be "mature." If confirmation is to be a mature affirmation of faith—if it is to persist as a Reformation-era "owning of the covenant"—then we can no longer confirm thirteen- or fifteen-year-olds who have completed six weeks of classes on Episcopal trivia. The renewal of baptismal vows is about the life-changing baptismal promises of Christian discipleship, and to make a mature, public affirmation of those vows is a demanding thing. As frustrating as it is for some, confirmation as it is currently constructed is simply not designed for children or adolescents.

At the same time, it would be wrong to make confirmation a ceremony celebrating completion of some prefabricated curriculum. While confirmation is a mature affirmation of baptism, there is no particular age at which confirmation should take place—only a minimum age prior to which confirmation makes a mockery of "mature affirmation." In other words, once one has reached the benchmark age of maturity (which I would suggest is at least eighteen), one might then choose to be confirmed—but only *might* choose to do so. It is crucial that the individual make the decision for her- or himself. It is unhelpful for a mature affirmation of faith to become just another step perfunctorily completed.

If confirmation functions as a mature affirmation of faith, reaffirmation of baptismal vows has a similar role. As we have discussed, the only variation from confirmation is the formula said over the candidate by the bishop and the lack of a rubric requiring the imposition of hands. Reaffirmation is, at its heart, simply a way for individuals publicly to recommit themselves to their baptism—and therefore it is not that different from confirmation. It is assumed that those who take part in reaffirmation have been previously confirmed (or received). It offers a way for adults to ritualize a milestone in their faith journeys. The rite of reaffirmation is the closest offspring of the single, repeatable rite "A Form for Confirmation or the Laying-On of Hands by the Bishop with the Affirmation of Baptismal Vows," found in *Prayer Book Studies 26*—the title of which misleadingly included confirmation, which was not otherwise mentioned in the rite. All of the internal references were to "Affirmation," and there were no variable options in the formulae used; the title's reference to confirmation had been inserted in the drafting process as *Prayer Book Studies 26* wended its way through various committees, and it was given its prominence by the General Convention.[25]

The great virtue of the reaffirmation rite is that it is repeatable, and therefore flexible. It might be used for those who were confirmed at age thirteen or fifteen and now perceive that they have come to a deeper faith (something done by many college students). It might be used for those who have "dropped out" of church for a time and have now returned, if they were previously confirmed by a bishop. In each of these cases, reaffirmation appropriately follows preparation, not unlike confirmation. Because this is a serious, public (re)commitment, it makes sense that the candidate should spend some time in prayer, study, and other formation before ritualizing this renewed commitment.

The Standing Liturgical Commission and the Theology and Prayer Book committees of the House of Bishops originally conceived of persons making a reaffirmation if they returned from a lapse in Christian life or if Christian life had become "perfunctory."[26] Yet in some places, persons have used it as they approach a personal milestone, such as parenthood, middle age, or retirement, without connecting it to a deepening of faith. Others have used it as they begin a new ministry or vocation. Both of these uses stretch the bounds of what was originally intended for the rite, although nothing in the BCP itself rules out such uses. In the latter case, of those beginning a new vocation or ministry, one should consider whether the "Form of Commitment to Christian Service" is more appropriate. For those who wish simply to mark a milestone, one might find appropriate options (depending upon the occasion) in the *Book of Occasional Services*. That said, some may find that a milestone in life or a new vocation really does cause their faith and Christian practice to be reinvigorated, and for these persons, the rite of reaffirmation is appropriate (after due preparation).

If the rite of reaffirmation is elastic, the rite of reception is rather narrower in its scope. As the prayer book frames it, the rite of reception is to be used for those entering the Episcopal Church from another faith tradition who would not be candidates for confirmation. It offers a way for those persons to ritualize this transition and to profess baptismal faith, which is then publicly recognized by their new community. It is important to note that just as in confirmation and reaffirmation, the candidates for reception renew their baptismal covenant. Reception is not, therefore, at its heart a pledge of membership, and there is no promise of loyalty to the Episcopal Church involved. One can only assume that this was a deliberate choice.

This stands in marked contrast to the rites used in other churches, especially in the Anglican Communion. The Anglican Church of Southern Africa, the Anglican Church of Kenya, the Anglican Church of Australia, and the Church of England, to name only a few, require the candidate to pledge loyalty to the denomination's discipline and teaching.[27] Such detailed questions do focus attention on the distinctive elements in Anglican faith and practice, which may foster a clearer sense of identity. But they also suggest more than a little anxiety on the part of the institutions that framed them. Further, none of the Anglican prayer books that ask such questions of candidates for reception also ask them of candidates for confirmation, suggesting that the anxiety is focused on the outsider coming into the church. The Episcopal Church (as well as the Anglican Church of Canada, for that matter) is notable for not binding such burdens on those coming to the church from other faith traditions.

What our rite of reception does entail is a renewal of baptismal vows, which the Episcopal Church (through the bishop and the assembly) recognizes as our common faith. The bishop's formula clearly sets this out: "N., we recognize you as a member of the one holy catholic and apostolic Church, and we receive you into the fellowship of this Communion. God, the Father, Son, and Holy Spirit, bless, preserve, and keep you."[28] This is not some sort of fraternity pledge, still less an oath of fealty, but a recognition of shared apostolic faith, which is sufficient basis for full communion.

The form of reception was itself a new thing in 1979. Previous prayer books had not included such a form, although precursors (such as Bishop Anthony Dopping's *A Form of Reconciliation of Lapsed Protestants and of Admission of Romanists to the Communion of the Church of Ireland*[29]) had existed and even been bound with some prayer books in the eighteenth century. These rites had been eclipsed by the use of confirmation for candidates from other churches, but a form of admission to communion, intended for those previously confirmed in other churches by bishops in the apostolic succession, was printed in the *Book of Offices* in 1949. The form of reception only entered the prayer book text late, in 1974, during the revisions of *Prayer Book Studies 26*, and it did so without ever being defined.[30] The history of this form suggests that it should be viewed as a variant of confirmation.

The inclusion of the form of reception complicated the question of how to incorporate new members from other denominations. The prayer book itself does not clarify for whom the rite of reception is appropriate, nor does it explicitly define confirmation, reception, and reaffirmation. There are scant clues in the opening rubrics stating the church's expectations of its members, which are themselves a revised version of an introductory rubric from *Prayer Book Studies 26*, designed for the single, repeatable rite of confirmation in that document.[31] These rubrics describe confirmation's essentials: 1) a mature, public affirmation of faith, 2) made in the presence of the bishop, 3) accompanied by the laying on of hands by that bishop.[32] Confirmation in other churches, if it lacks these components, is not confirmation as the prayer book defines it, and therefore a prayer book purist would argue that persons from those other churches should be confirmed, not received. For example, a former Presbyterian who was confirmed in that church should be confirmed in the Episcopal Church, because his public affirmation of faith was not made in the presence of a bishop, and he did not receive a bishop's imposition of hands. A former Roman Catholic, baptized as an infant and confirmed at age ten, would need to be confirmed in the Episcopal Church, because while she received the imposition of hands from a bishop, she did not make a *mature* affirmation of faith. A former Roman Catholic who was baptized in that church as an adult in the Rite of Christian Initiation of Adults (RCIA) would need to be confirmed, because adult baptismal candidates are confirmed immediately after baptism by the parish pastor—a priest—in the RCIA liturgy. Finally, a former member of one of the Eastern Orthodox churches would need to be confirmed, because those churches practice infant chrismation, done by a presbyter, and not anything resembling the Western rite of confirmation. Thus, under the BCP (interpreted strictly), it would appear that the rite of reception would be quite rarely used.

Beginning not long after the new prayer book was given final approval, the church began to revise its canons to address the question of whom to confirm and whom to receive.[33] The present canons (of 2009) directly contradict the prayer book's position, if construed strictly: canon I.17(c) states,

> It is expected that all adult members of this Church, after appropriate instruction, will have made a mature public affirmation of their faith and commitment to the responsibilities of their Baptism and will have been confirmed or received by the laying on of hands by a Bishop of this Church or by a Bishop of a Church in communion with this Church. Those who have previously made a mature public commitment in another Church may be received by the laying on of hands by a Bishop of this Church, rather than confirmed.[34]

After restating the book's expectation that adult members will have made a "mature public affirmation of faith" and "will have been confirmed or received" by a bishop of this church, the canon then contradicts the BCP. If one has made a mature commitment in another church, regardless of the presence of a bishop, one may then be received, not confirmed, in this church. The argument, presumably, is that the essential element in confirmation is the profession of faith, not the presence of a bishop—which is not the position of the BCP. Under this canon, the Presbyterian confirmed in that church or the Roman Catholic adult who was baptized and confirmed according to RCIA would both be received, not confirmed, while the Roman Catholic confirmed at age ten would be confirmed again (because of the lack of a mature affirmation).

Unfortunately the next section of the canon then clouds the issue further. Canon I.17(d) addresses the question of adults baptized in this church:

> (d) Any person who is baptized in this Church as an adult and receives the laying on of hands by the Bishop at Baptism is to be considered, for the purpose of this and all other Canons, as both baptized and confirmed; also,
>
> Any person who is baptized in this Church as an adult and at some time after the Baptism receives the laying on of hands by the Bishop in Reaffirmation of Baptismal Vows is to be considered, for the purpose of this and all other Canons, as both baptized and confirmed;

The first part of the section is quite clear: those baptized in the Episcopal Church as adults by a bishop, who then imposes hands at the consignation, need not be confirmed. But the second part of the section addresses those baptized in the Episcopal Church as adults by a presbyter: they need not be confirmed, but may undergo the "reaffirmation of baptismal vows." Since the only thing distinguishing the rite of reaffirmation from that of confirmation is the formula used at the hand-laying, it is not at all clear what this is meant to accomplish.

The third and final section of I.17(d) more sharply departs from the narrow construction of the prayer book:

> Any baptized person who received the laying on of hands at Confirmation (by any Bishop in apostolic succession) and is received into the Episcopal Church by a Bishop of this Church is to be considered, for the purpose of this and all other Canons, as both baptized and confirmed.[35]

This section appears to drop the expectation that one to be received should have made a prior, mature affirmation of faith. Accordingly, the hypothetical former Roman Catholic confirmed at age ten by a bishop in that church would be received, not confirmed, despite the fact that Roman confirmation is a very different thing than the Episcopal rite that shares the same name.

Only those entering the Episcopal Church from the Eastern Orthodox tradition would appear to still require confirmation, since the Orthodox do not have a rite resembling confirmation, only infant chrismation at baptism. Since the Orthodox do not make a mature profession of faith, and no bishop imposes hands at the chrismation (which is done by a presbyter), the canons do not appear to leave room for them to be received.

There are two valid approaches to this confusion. One is to consider the Book of Common Prayer as ambiguous and the canons as the church's official gloss on it. By this approach, one would tend to receive most converts, reserving confirmation to those who have never made either a mature affirmation of faith *or* experienced anything that could loosely be described, by some stretch of the term, as confirmation. The other approach is to see the prayer book as the higher formulary, and therefore to maintain the prayer book approach (construed strictly), which is to see confirmation as a mature affirmation of faith accompanied by the bishop's imposition of hands. Absent both of these elements, one has not experienced prayer book confirmation and must therefore be confirmed. Either approach is reasonable, given the confusion around confirmation and reception; the best counsel for parish clergy is to follow the norms of their diocese and to hope for future prayer book revision to resolve the confusion.

ENACTING CONFIRMATION

All of these elements of the BCP's approach to confirmation should guide its liturgical performance. The rite assumes that the candidates are previously baptized adults, who have been properly prepared to renew their baptismal vows. The staging of the rite needs to support the prayer book's view of confirmation, and by extension its view of baptism, for confirmation exists solely as a derivative, and subordinate, rite to baptism.

One way to make this derivative nature clear would be to schedule baptisms only at the bishop's visit and at the Easter Vigil, thus making it more likely that confirmation would not take place apart from a baptism in the average congregation. Then, within the rite, it would be important to make sure that the candidates for confirmation, reception, and reaffirmation do not displace or steal attention from the candidates for baptism. By celebrating baptism and confirmation at the same liturgy, a bishop and congregation would place confirmation in its proper theological and liturgical context.

Whether celebrated together with baptism or apart, as Aidan Kavanagh observed, "confirmation should not be made too much over," and certainly it should never be elevated to the rank of baptism or eucharist.[36] Confirmation is often susceptible to ceremonial inflation. Baptism and eucharist may be presided over by a garden-variety presbyter, while only a bishop may confirm in the Episcopal Church; eucharist happens each week (or should!), baptism can happen several times a year, but confirmation happens only when the bishop is in town; confirmation, unlike infant baptism and reception of the eucharist, requires preparation of the candidate. Each is a factor in the distortion of confirmation into something that appears more special than it really is. Liturgical leaders must consciously work to undermine these factors of "specialness" and keep confirmation in its subordinate position. In short, Kavanagh was right: we shouldn't fuss too much over it.

As part of maintaining clarity about the relative place of baptism, confirmation, and confirmation's cognate rites, there needs to be careful thought about the use of chrism. I will argue in a later chapter that the optional chrismation in baptism should always be performed, as an important part of the restoration of the baptismal liturgy along the lines of the early church's rites. But while Cranmer omitted chrism from Anglican confirmation in 1549, in contrast to medieval and contemporary Roman confirmation (where it remained the essential part of the rite), many Episcopal bishops have come to use it in confirmation. It is likely that the custom has roots in the Anglo-Catholic movement of the nineteenth and twentieth centuries, and its use is documented in surveys of bishops' procedures.[37] This follows present-day Roman use, which continues to use chrism in confirmation.[38] The best argument in favor of the practice is that offered by Paul Marshall, who notes that chrismation is repeatable in the East, and that chrism serves as "a sign of each baptized person's identity with *messiach*." Therefore, chrismation may be repeated "whenever baptismal vows are solemnly renewed before the bishop," in confirmation, reception, or reaffirmation (alike).[39] I would be more cautious, believing that repeating chrismation in confirmation, because of the rite's history, risks a liturgical and historical confusion. Chrismation was deliberately restored to the baptismal rite in 1979 in order to reassemble the ancient rite of initiation; chrismating at confirmation risks obscuring that reunified rite. Further, Eastern chrismation is not *normally* done apart from baptism, except in the case of receiving converts who were not previously chrismated, and it is not normally repeated, except in the case of apostates who have returned to the faith, weakening the precedent cited for chrismation at confirmation.[40] Provided that the later chrismations are framed as a recalling of the first chrismation at baptism, and provided chrism is also used at each and every reception and reaffirmation of baptismal vows, and any other solemn renewal of baptismal vows (such as the prayer book's "Form of Commitment to Christian Service"), the use of chrism at confirmation might be tolerated. For that matter, even in baptism itself chrismation should be seen as only an amplification and elaboration of the basic act, which is the washing in water. Nevertheless, I would argue for the restriction of chrismation to baptism alone.

In the performance of the liturgy, great care should be taken so that confirmation, reception, and reaffirmation are ritualized in the same way. The 1979 BCP (not to mention the canons) equate the three in almost every respect: each is a solemn, mature renewal of baptismal promises before the bishop. They are only distinguishable by variations in the bishop's formulae, each of which nevertheless asks God's blessing on the candidate and invokes the Holy Spirit in some way. This means that candidates for any of the three rites should be treated identically. The bishop should impose hands on each one of them—the ancient gesture of prayer and blessing over a person, never restricted to confirmation. This will be a new practice in several places: some bishops have been known to shake hands with candidates for reception and reaffirmation, which is hardly as evocative or powerful a gesture as the imposition of hands. The formula for each of the rites involves a request for God's blessing, and the more ancient gesture of blessing is the imposition of hands, so it really is best to impose hands in all three rites.

Finally, while the prayer book makes provisions for the rite of confirmation apart from a celebration of the eucharist, one should at all costs avoid such a liturgical aberration. Historically, Anglican divines argued that through participation in the eucharist, one renews one's baptism. This thematic element in the eucharist helps support the mature affirmation (or reaffirmation) that we currently see confirmation and its cognates to be. Indeed, it does so far more powerfully than confirmation itself. Apart from the eucharist, the confirmation rite is an odd little squib of a rite, cut loose from sacramental moorings, and generally unsatisfying in its shape and performance.

The present prayer book, then, reserves a small but distinctive role for confirmation, reception, and reaffirmation. Framed simply as a public affirmation (or reaffirmation) of baptismal promises, it has been stripped of much of its past glory. In its enactment, we need to be mindful of its modest scope and to avoid doing anything that would over-ritualize it, distorting its place in the sacramental economy.

Notes

1. Meyers, *Continuing the Reformation*, 147–87.

2. Kavanagh, *Confirmation*, 3–72.

3. BCP 1979, 418–19.

4. William Gregg acknowledges this perspective in his list of questions raised by confirmation practice. William O. Gregg, "Introduction: On Confirmation," in Theology Committee of the House of Bishops, *Forming Christians: Reflections on Baptism, Confirmation, and Christian Formation* (2005), 11.

5. Henry N. Parsley Jr., "Further Thoughts on a Theology of Confirmation," in *Forming Christians*, 31.

6. For the appeal to unity, see J. Robert Wright, "*Prayer Book Studies 26*: Considered Objections," *Anglican Theological Review* 57 (1975): 61, 66, 71; for the anticongregational claim, see Donald Parsons, "Some Theological and Pastoral Implications of Confirmation," in Cully, ed., *Confirmation Re-Examined*, 51.

7. For example, Leonel L. Mitchell, "The Theology of Christian Initiation and the Proposed Book of Common Prayer," *Anglican Theological Review* 60 (1978): 413.

8. Parsley, "Further Thoughts," 31; A. Katherine Grieb and Robert W. Ihloff, "The Bishop's Role in Catechetical Formation: A Proposal for 'Best Practices' to Be Implemented at the Diocesan and Parish Levels of the Church," in *Forming Christians*, 48–50.

9. Parsley, "Further Thoughts," 31; on the faults in this line of argument, see James F. Turrell, "Muddying the Waters of Baptism: The Theology Committee's Report on Baptism, Confirmation, and Christian Formation," *Anglican Theological Review* 88 (2006): 346–50.

10. BCP 1979, 308.

11. Kathryn Tanner, "Towards a New Theology of Confirmation," *Anglican Theological Review* 88 (2006): 34.

12. BCP, 304–5.

13. *Rite of Christian Initiation of Adults*, study ed. (Collegeville, MN: Liturgical Press, 1988) [henceforth, RCIA], 20; Aidan Kavanagh, "Catechesis: Formation in Stages," in *The Baptismal Mystery and the Catechumenate,* ed. Michael W. Merriman (New York: Church Hymnal Corporation, 1990), 43–44; Kavanagh, *Shape of Baptism*, 130; *The Book of Occasional Services 2003* (New York: Church Publishing, 2004) [henceforth, BOS], 116.

14. BCP 1979, 412.

15. *Oxford English Dictionary*, 3rd ed. March 2001; online version June 2012, *http://0-www. oed.com.catalog.sewanee.edu/view/Entry/115114*, accessed June 26, 2012; *Webster's Third New International Dictionary, Unabridged, http://0-gateway.proquest.com.catalog.sewanee.edu/openurl/ openurl?ctx_ver=Z39.88-2003&xri:pqil:res_ver=0.2&res_id=xri:ilcs-us&rft_id=xri:ilcs:ft:web sters:Z200995277:2*, accessed June 26, 2012.

16. On Episcopal practices, Iris Cully, "Aspects of Childhood Confirmation" in Cully, ed., *Confirmation Re-Examined*, 93; Urban T. Holmes, "Confirmation as a Rite of Intensification: A Response to J. Robert Wright," *Anglican Theological Review* 57 (1975): 75; on Roman norms, Kavanagh, *Confirmation*, 97–101; Grieb and Ihloff, "The Bishop's Role in Catechetical Formation," 49.

17. Holmes, "Confirmation as a Rite of Intensification," 75.

18. Kali H. Trzesniewski, M. Brent Donnellan, and Richard W. Robins, "Stability of Self-Esteem across the Life Span," *Journal of Personality and Social Psychology* 84 (2003): 216.

19. Holmes, "Confirmation as a Rite of Intensification," 75; John W. Santrock, *Children*, 9th ed. (Boston: McGraw-Hill, 2007), 44–47; Michael Green and John A. Piel, *Theories of Human Development: A Comparative Approach* (Boston: Allyn and Bacon, 2002), 89, 303–6, 310. William Crain, *Theories of Development: Concepts and Applications*, 4th ed. (Upper Saddle River, NJ: Prentice Hall, 2000), 158–59.

20. James W. Fowler, *Stages of Faith: The Psychology of Human Development and the Quest for Meaning* (San Francisco: HarperCollins, 1981), 122–213.

21. For example, the pioneer of the influential theory of "multiple intelligences," Howard Gardner, notes that individuals achieve higher-order skills in their multiple intelligences at different times, and Howard Boom's "taxonomy of learning" has been sharply critiqued for its implicit assumption of linear progression through stages in a "cumulative hierarchy." Howard Gardner, *Frames of Mind: The Theory of Multiple Intelligences* (New York: Basic Books, 1983); Howard Gardner, *Multiple Intelligences: New Horizons*, rev. ed. (New York: Basic Books, 2006); Edward J. Furst, "Bloom's Taxonomy: Philosophical and Educational Issues," in *Bloom's Taxonomy: A Forty-Year Retrospective*, ed. Lorin W. Anderson and Lauren A. Sosniak (Chicago: National Society for the Study of Education, 1994), 34–35;

William D. Rohwer, Jr., and Kathryn Sloane, "Psychological Perspectives" in Anderson and Sosniak, eds., *Bloom's Taxonomy*, 47; Lorin W. Anderson, David R. Krathwohl et al., *A Taxonomy for Learning, Teaching, and Assessing: A Revision of Boom's Taxonomy of Educational Objectives*, complete ed. (New York: Longman, 1983), 293.

22. BCP 1979, 412.

23. Sofia Cavalletti, *The Religious Potential of the Child: Experiencing Scripture and Liturgy with Young Children*, trans. Patricia M. Coulter and Julie M. Coulter (Chicago: Liturgy Training Publications, 1992), 21–45, 151–56; on the capacity of children to engage in worship, see also "The Directory for Masses with Children," in Gabe Huck, ed., *Leader's Manual: Hymnal for Catholic Students* (Chicago: Liturgy Training Publications, 1989), 111–12.

24. Teresa M. McDevitt and Jeanne Ellis Ormrod, *Child Development: Educating and Working with Children and Adolescents*, 2nd ed. (Upper Saddle River, NJ: Pearson, 2004), 437–39, 444; Judy Dunn, "The Beginnings of Moral Understanding: Development in the Second Year," in *The Emergence of Morality in Young Children*, ed. Jerome Kagan and Sharon Lamb (Chicago: University of Chicago Press, 1990), 91–112; Catherine Snow, "Comment: Language and the Beginnings of Moral Understanding," in Kagan and Lamb, eds., *Emergence of Morality*, 112–22.

25. Standing Liturgical Commission, *Holy Baptism: Together with a Form for the Affirmation of Baptismal Vows with the Laying-On of Hands by the Bishop, Also Called Confirmation* (New York: Church Hymnal Corporation, 1973) [henceforth, *PBS 26*]; Meyers, *Continuing the Reformation*, 174–77.

26. Hatchett, *Commentary*, 273.

27. The Church of the Province of Southern Africa, *An Anglican Prayer Book 1989* (Jeppestown: Collins Liturgical Publications, 1989), 399–400; Anglican Church of Kenya, *Our Modern Services* (Nairobi: Uzima Press, 2002), 65; Anglican Church of Australia, *A Prayer Book for Australia* (Mulgrave, Victoria: Broughton Books, 1999), 96; Church of England, *Common Worship: Christian Initiation* (London: Church House Publishing, 2006), 215–17.

28. BCP 1979, 418.

29. Anthony Dopping, *A Form of Reconciliation of Lapsed Protestants and of Admission of Romanists to the Communion of the Church of Ireland* (Dublin: Andrew Crook, 1691).

30. Hatchett, *Commentary*, 272; Meyers, *Continuing the Reformation*, 81, 181–83.

31. *PBS 26*, 22.

32. BCP 1979, 412.

33. Revisions took place in 1985 and 1997. Meyers, *Continuing the Reformation*, 243–45; The Episcopal Church Office of Ecumenical and Interfaith Relations, "Guidelines for Reception and Confirmation for Persons Joining the Episcopal Church," accessed June 21, 2012, at *http://archive.episcopalchurch.org/documents/confirmation.pdf*.

34. The Episcopal Church, *Constitution and Canons Together with the Rules of Order for the Government of the Protestant Episcopal Church in the United States of America Otherwise Known as The Episcopal Church* (New York: Church Publishing, 2009) [henceforth, *Constitution and Canons*], I.17(c).

35. *Constitution and Canons*, I.17(d).

36. Kavanagh, *Confirmation*, 117.

37. Ruth Meyers notes a 1986 survey [Meyers, *Continuing the Reformation*, 239]. A survey in 2005 showed that 42 of 101 responding bishops used chrism in confirmation ["Questionnaire Responses by the House of Bishops Spring Meeting 2005," in *Forming Christians*, 70–73].

38. International Commission on English in the Liturgy, *The Rites of the Catholic Church*, vol. 1 (Collegeville, MN: Liturgical Press, 1990), 490–91.

39. Paul V. Marshall, *The Bishop Is Coming!: A Practical Guide for Bishops and Congregations* (New York: Church Publishing, 2007), 37–38.

40. Paul Turner, *Confirmation: The Baby in Solomon's Court*, rev. ed. (Chicago: Liturgical Training Publications, 2006), 24; Christine Hall, "The Use of Holy Oils in the Orthodox Churches of the Byzantine Tradition," in *The Oil of Gladness: Anointing in the Christian Tradition*, ed. Martin Dudley and Geoffrey Rowell (Collegeville, MN: Liturgical Press, 1993), 102, 111 n3.

Chapter 3

CATECHUMENAL RITES AND FORMATION

While the ethos of the 1979 BCP is structured around baptism, the prayer book itself does not address the prebaptismal formation of candidates beyond a minimalist rubric requiring that adult candidates and the sponsors of infant candidates receive "preparation." Adult candidates will need one sort of formation, delivered before their baptisms. Infant candidates will need a very different sort of formation, in order to live into the baptism that others willed for them to receive. It would be nonsensical to expect that the same sort of preparation could work for both. A third group of persons also needs preparation for ritual promises: candidates for confirmation, reception, or reaffirmation of baptismal vows. Although those rites are, at root, a mature affirmation of faith and not a mark of completion of some educational program, the candidates need to be able to make an informed assent to the baptismal covenant. Candidates for these rites need to be given the support of the church to take the step of renewing these vows: only then can they with full knowledge commit themselves to what the baptismal vows really mean for their lives.

The *Book of Occasional Services* offers outlines for three processes of preparation. One is a revival of the ancient catechumenate, for the preparation of adult candidates for baptism. The BOS borrowed heavily from the Roman Catholic Church's *Rite of Christian Initiation of Adults*. The other two processes are themselves modeled on the catechumenate, though pains are taken to avoid describing the candidates undergoing the processes as "catechumens," reserving that term for the unbaptized. One such catechumenal process is designed to prepare candidates for confirmation, reception, and reaffirmation, while the other is intended to prepare parents and godparents of infant candidates for baptism.

Each of these processes is punctuated by various ceremonies that are inserted into the Sunday liturgy as the candidates reach certain milestones in their preparation. The mile-marker rites for the catechumenate and those for the process of preparation of confirmands follow the cycle of the church year. The

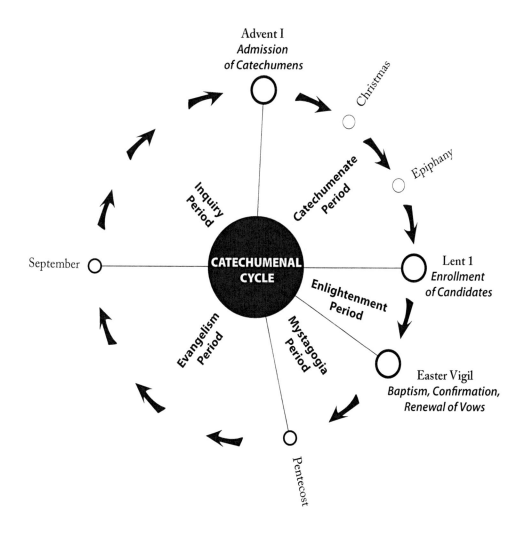

catechumenate begins with the "inquiry" period, running until the First Sunday of Advent. The process then enters the "catechumenate" phase, strictly defined. The next phase, of "candidacy for baptism" or "enlightenment," begins at the First Sunday of Lent. The final stage, of "mystagogia" (or post-baptismal instruction), follows after baptism at the Great Vigil of Easter. The mileposts outlined in the *Book of Occasional Services* for the process leading to confirmation, reception, or reaffirmation include Ash Wednesday and Maundy Thursday. The process of preparation of parents and godparents for infant candidates is not tied to the church year in the same way, because it is framed around the birth of the child.

ADULT BAPTISMAL CANDIDATES AND FORMATION

The catechumenate was the early church's model of preparation. It varied in its length and other details according to time and place, but in essence it was a period of formation and examination of adult baptismal candidates. The catechumenate was not ordered around teaching a body of doctrine, but aimed at training candidates in the Christian life.[1]

The Apostolic Tradition (which has been dated variously from the early third century to the late fourth century) is one of the earliest sources for the catechumenate. It describes a lengthy catechumenate of three years. Newcomers were first examined as to their manner of life, with certain crafts and professions being forbidden. If they passed this scrutiny, they would be admitted as catechumens. They would gather for instruction and would pray, as a group, apart from the worshipping assembly. At the conclusion of each session, they would be dismissed with the imposition of hands by the teacher. As the day for their baptism drew near, the catechumens would be examined to see if they had lived virtuously, and then prayed over and exorcised. They would spend the night before baptism in prayer and fasting, and then be baptized at the Easter Vigil.[2] While the catechumenate in other places could be shorter, it remained a period of scrutiny and formation for the baptism that followed.

After the disappearance of the catechumenate in the Middle Ages, the Protestant and Catholic Reformations injected a new emphasis on education (under the heading of "catechizing"). Their approaches were markedly different from that of the ancient catechumenate. Instead of training disciples, the churches emphasized the mastery of a body of doctrine. This shift in the sixteenth century carried over well into the twentieth, with the ubiquitous "confirmation class" as its legacy.

But rather than mastering a body of intellectual precepts, the truly unchurched person needs a basic grounding in Christianity, which is a Way, not a body of doctrine (as important as doctrine may be). This requires a sort of immersion experience (forgive the pun), not least because baptism is a life-changing sacrament that places demands on the whole person: on her thought, lifestyle, actions, and choices. To address this need, the catechumenate was revived by Roman Catholic missionaries in some parts of Africa in the eighteenth century, experimented with in Western dioceses in the 1950s and 1960s, and restored to widespread use in the Roman Catholic Church in the Rite of Christian Initiation of Adults in 1972.[3] The catechumenate in RCIA has several significant features. It is designed as a parish-based effort, with both clergy and laity providing leadership. In addition, "[t]he entire community must help the candidates and the catechumens throughout the process of initiation,"[4] aiding all the parish community to reflect on their own faith journeys.

After experiments in several Episcopal parishes, the denomination as a whole adopted a format for the catechumenate in the first edition of the *Book of Occasional Services*. It has been refined and elaborated in subsequent editions. The overall structure of the BOS catechumenate is quite similar to the RCIA structure, with three stages culminating in baptism. While the specific content of the instruction during the catechumenate is not set out, the BOS gives the basic principles, with an emphasis on the practice of reflection on experience.[5]

PREPARATION OF CANDIDATES FOR CONFIRMATION/ RECEPTION/REAFFIRMATION

Adult baptismal candidates are not as familiar a sight in Episcopal parishes as one might wish, but confirmands are ubiquitous. How, then, should these candidates be prepared? The usual solution in Episcopal parishes is the "confirmation class," a model of preparation that often focuses on an academic style of learning: mastery of a body of knowledge through talks by clergy or lay leaders, sometimes supplemented by reading assignments. The content covered in the "confirmation class" may cover a range of topics, often drawing on the catechism in the back of the BCP, but it often includes a heavy dose of material focused on the distinctive aspects of the Episcopal Church.

Efforts to turn the confirmation class into a short course in Anglican identity, however well intentioned, are misguided. As noted in chapter 2, the rite of reception in the 1979 prayer book pointedly omits the oaths of allegiance to Anglicanism included in other Anglican churches' equivalent rites; reception is instead based on recognition of baptismal faith. The Episcopal Church's rite of confirmation similarly includes no such promise of fealty or allegiance. The 1979 BCP makes it clear that confirmation is not about denominational identity; it is an affirmation of baptismal faith, which is to say, *Christian* faith. Confirmation preparation will, of course, present the Christian faith as seen through Anglican/Episcopal lenses, but it will be much more than a sort of crash course in EpiscoTrivia.

Because confirmation is really about renewal of baptismal promises, preparation should be about the living of the Christian life, not merely the mastery of a body of knowledge. That may mean, in some parishes, a fundamental reorientation of the mode of preparation, as well as a change in the content that is conveyed. The best option available for formation of those intending to renew their baptismal promises in confirmation, reception, or reaffirmation is a process very much like the catechumenate for candidates for baptism. Each edition of the *Book of Occasional Services* has been quite clear: the catechumenate is reserved for adult candidates for baptism. The church published, in the 1988 revision of the *Book of Occasional Services*, an adaptation of the catechumenal process for the preparation of persons for confirmation and its cognate rites, as well as another adaptation for the preparation of parents and godparents of infant candidates for baptism. These have been fine-tuned in subsequent editions.[6] While these processes avoid using the term "catechumen" to describe their candidates and the "milepost" rites are different, they follow the same basic structure of the catechumenate. It is theologically important to distinguish the unbaptized, as "true" catechumens, from those baptized persons who are deepening their faith commitment—one's baptism is full and complete initiation, and it is indissoluble. But from a practical standpoint, the process of the catechumenate is a powerful means of preparing these baptized persons. Some parishes combine the unbaptized catechumens and baptized candidates for confirmation in the same catechumenal process, which offers advantages by ensuring critical mass for the program.

Regardless of whether a parish uses two separate tracks or a combined approach, the catechumenal process is an effective means for preparing candidates for confirmation, reception, and reaffirmation. It avoids the faults of the typical "confirmation class," which is generally overly academic and lecture driven, and too likely to detour into Anglican and Episcopal trivia at the expense of more vital matters. Christianity is a practice, not a body of doctrine, and the catechumenal process is the best approach available for preparing persons to live the Christian life. It works for these candidates for the same reasons that it works for the unbaptized catechumens: by pairing candidates with sponsors; creating supportive small groups; and addressing the whole of Christian life, from belief to practice.

INFANT BAPTISM AND FORMATION

The presence of infant candidates complicates the theology and performance of the baptismal rite, with its serious emphasis on discipleship and its recitation of the baptismal covenant. There is some cognitive dissonance inherent in the juxtaposition of the two. Writing on the reformed rites of the Second Vatican Council, Aidan Kavanagh has helpfully observed that the norm of baptism in the Roman Catholic Church is adult baptism of candidates who have undergone a significant period of preparation in the catechumenate. A norm, he reminds us, is not the same thing as the conventional pattern: "A norm in this sense has nothing to do with the number of times a thing is done, but it has everything to do with the standard according to which a thing is done."[7] Other sorts of candidates may be baptized, and their baptism is not ineffective or illegitimate. But the baptism of infants is, in Kavanagh's analysis, a benign abnormality so long as it is practiced with prudence as an unavoidable pastoral necessity—in situations such as the frail health of the infant, or in response to the earnest desire of Christian parents whose faith is vigorous and whose way of life gives clear promise that their child will develop in the faith of the Church. But at the same time, tradition's witness to adult baptism as the norm provides a solid counterbalance against infant baptism's becoming a malign abnormality due to pastoral malfeasance, theological obsession, or the decline of faith among Christian parents into some degree of merely social conformity.[8]

Paradoxically, by giving shape to the rite, the norm of adult baptism allows infant baptism to function appropriately within the household of faith. The same approach helps in examining the 1979 prayer book's rites: adult baptism is the norm that gives shape to the rite, but infant baptism is still legitimate, though not the norm.

Given that a baby of a few months' age is not in a position to undertake a period of study and formation before baptism, the question, then, is what sort of formation they should receive after they have been initiated. This must proceed on two tracks—church based and home based—as it is unrealistic to think that the church can inculcate Christian practices and beliefs in children without a partnership with family members.

Parents bringing children for baptism should have some sort of relationship to the church. The query posed in the baptismal liturgy to the congregation, asking if they will support the candidates in their new life in Christ, indicates the need for some sort of engagement by parents in the church's life, since otherwise the congregation could not make that pledge of support without fear of perjury.

One might plausibly offer the "Thanksgiving for the Birth or Adoption of a Child" to those who are more interested in a celebration for an infant than in bringing up a full-bore disciple. As a rite, it is more like the medieval "Churching of Women" than a rite marking a stage in the journey to baptism. But for parents who seek a ritual acknowledging a new baby without the theological content of baptism, it might serve. One would use the prayer "For a child not yet baptized" at page 444. In any case, it offers a ritual substitute without the heavy commitment of either baptism or enrollment of the child as a catechumen.

The *Book of Occasional Services* provides a pattern of preparation, "The Preparation of Parents and Godparents for the Baptism of Infants and Young Children" (page 159). Modeled along the lines of the catechumenate for adult candidates (discussed below), it has parents and godparents reflect on their experience in light of the baptismal covenant and the life of faith, as well as exploring the obligations of parents and godparents. The book recommends that persons who have raised children in the church might serve as resources for those going through the process of preparation.[9]

The only way that children baptized as infants will be raised in the Christian faith and life (as promised in the liturgy) is for their parents or guardians to inculcate those values in them as they grow up. Parents need to be equipped by the church to do this, through a program of formation that will in turn enable them to form the child. Additionally, because the assent of faith required in baptism of adults has, for infants, been made by the parents and sponsors, those adults need to be able to make an informed assent. As further support, the church must then offer serious formation to these infants as they grow up. What begins as baptismal preparation for the parents and godparents of infant candidates, then, is really just the first stage in a lifelong pattern for those infants as they grow up in the church.

PREPARATION OF PARENTS OF INFANT CANDIDATES FOR BAPTISM

The formation process for parents and godparents in the *Book of Occasional Services* establishes a foundation for this ongoing, cooperative work. Modeled on the catechumenate, it too is a multistage process, with rituals to punctuate transitions between stages. The first stage begins with the start of pregnancy. In it, parents consult with the local pastor, plan subsequent meetings, and choose godparents for their child (and the guidelines are clear that at least one godparent should be from the local community). It ends with a brief rite that takes place either privately or in the public liturgy, the "Blessing of Parents at the Beginning of the Pregnancy." In the second stage, which lasts until birth, the parents and godparents meet regularly with catechists, exploring "salvation history, prayer, worship, and social ministry," through a model of reflection on experience. Shortly after the birth of the child, the stage ends with the "Thanksgiving for the Birth or Adoption of a Child," ordinarily within the public liturgy. In the third and final stage, parents and godparents continue to meet with catechists, as well as with others who have raised children in the faith, and they explore ways of providing age-appropriate formation and education to their children (such as "the best way to interpret the meaning of the Eucharist to a child" and "ways of introducing the child to the story of salvation"). The process then culminates in baptism, on one of the baptismal occasions specified in the prayer book. There is no post-baptismal catechesis *per se*; rather, it is expected that "the parents, godparents, and congregation have the responsibility of carrying out the child's formation."[10]

This catechumenal process is also highly adaptable. It could be done informally in a smaller parish, where there is not likely to be more than one pregnancy at a time, or in a more structured, formal way in larger parishes. It provides an option for Christian parents who might want to defer their child's baptism, to allow her or him to make more of a conscious choice. In such a case, the preparatory process culminates not in baptism but in the enrollment of the infant as a catechumen. The child will then grow up, participate in pre-baptismal formation, and decide whether to proceed to baptism.[11]

While the *Book of Occasional Services* does not anticipate such a thing except in the case of an unbaptized parent, the process of preparing parents and godparents could also be combined with the catechumenate, much as with the preparation of adults for confirmation/reception/reaffirmation. In such a combined process, one might need to provide time and space for "true" catechumens and parents each to get their own needs met, through break-out sessions or additional meetings for parents around child-rearing concerns. The catechumenate is supposed to be home-cooked, so this adaptation is not unprecedented. Because the catechumenate is meant to build on local gifts and talents to meet local needs, there is ample room for overlapping or combining the catechumenal processes for the three different groups of catechumens, candidates for reaffirmation rites, and parents and godparents.

Of course, these categories themselves will sometimes overlap. The birth of a child is frequently a point of re-entry for Episcopalians who have drifted from the church, as well as for those who are unchurched or those from another tradition who have decided to find a new church home. In this context, the beauty of the catechumenal process is its heavy emphasis on listening and the sharing of stories, as participants reflect on how their stories and God's story intersect. This provides a respectful, nonthreatening environment that can invite persons in, not scare them away. While catechumenate is, in some respects, a "high demand" process, requiring an investment of time and energy on the part of participants who wish to undergo the rites of initiation, it is at the same time a gentle process when done well.

"AND NOW, A WORD ABOUT OUR SPONSORS . . ."

In each catechumenal process and in the liturgy of baptism, there is an explicit role for sponsors. The prayer book does not say much concerning the choice of baptismal sponsors, other than that they are to be baptized persons. Regarding their role and preparation, the baptismal rite stipulates that sponsors of adults and older children "signify their endorsement of the candidates and their intention to support them by prayer and example in their Christian life," while "sponsors of infants . . . make promises in their own names, and also take vows on behalf of their candidates." The prayer book requires preparation of sponsors of infants ("in the nature and meaning of Baptism, in their duties to help the new Christians grow in the knowledge and love of God, and in their responsibilities as members of his Church"), but it prescribes no preparation for sponsors of adult candidates. The *Book of Occasional Services* adds nothing further concerning the sponsors of adult candidates, beyond the expectation that sponsors in the catechumenate will be prepared for their liturgical roles in the "milepost" rites of transition, and that sponsors of those reaffirming their baptismal vows will be drawn from the local congregation. There is at least a bit more information concerning the preparation of sponsors for infant candidates, as sketched in the section above, and the BOS also indicates that at least one sponsor of an infant candidate for baptism should come from the local community.[12]

These guidelines regarding sponsors of infant candidates, if they are taken seriously, will cause a substantial change in the way that many godparents are chosen. Many parents select godparents from among relatives and friends, who are often geographically quite far-flung. The *Book of Occasional Services* does not rule out including such godparents, but it does insist that at least one godparent be in the local community. It is most helpful to read this as meaning, "local ecclesial community," meaning the parish, although nothing precludes one from reading this as allowing for a baptized Christian in the town or village who is not resident in the same parish community. The reason for the insistence on one local godparent has a great deal to do with the godparents' promises to "be responsible for seeing that the child . . . is brought up in the Christian faith and life" and through "prayers and witness [to] help this child to grow into the full stature of Christ."[13] It can be difficult to do such things from a geographic remove. Distant godparents also deprive the child of another example of Christian faith and life.

CEREMONIAL GUIDE TO THE RITES OF THE CATECHUMENAL PROCESSES

What follows are some practical suggestions about implementing the simple "mile-marker" rites in the *Book of Occasional Services* 2003 for the catechumenate. The directions could be adapted fairly easily for the catechumenal rites for those preparing for the renewal of baptismal vows, if the parish runs the two processes separately.

The BOS rites for those seeking confirmation/reception/reaffirmation retain the penitential flavor of their Roman Catholic roots. In one case, the Maundy Thursday "rite of preparation" for those seeking confirmation/reception/reaffirmation, the penitential flavor is even stronger, because the model was the ancient church's solemn reconciliation of penitents, according to the chair of the drafting committee.[14]

This borrowing is problematic. In the contemporary Episcopal Church, the only basis for exclusion of the baptized from communion are the disciplinary rubrics of the prayer book. Those rubrics limit excommunication (for that is what it is) to those who are guilty of notorious evil. This means that those baptized persons joining the Episcopal Church from some other tradition, those raised in the church who now seek confirmation, and even the vast majority of those who fell away from the church and are now coming back to seek the reaffirmation of baptismal vows should not be treated like the Roman Catholic order of penitents. Certainly they should not be excluded from the eucharist. The survival of extensive penitential language and imagery in these rites makes them a poor choice for most of the persons who will seek confirmation/reception/reaffirmation. While the rites are discussed below, it is important to consider alternatives.

In the material below, *italicized* text gives directions, while the roman type following gives commentary.

ADMISSION OF CATECHUMENS

The admission of catechumens takes place at the principal eucharist on the First Sunday of Advent.

While the rubrics allow the rite of admission to take place at any time of year, the First Sunday of Advent offers enough lead time before the Easter Vigil to work well. In parishes that are combining in the same catechumenal process preparation of those seeking baptism and those seeking confirmation/reception/reaffirmation, care is taken to distinguish the two groups at the rite of admission. For the latter group, the BOS assumes that the rite of "Welcoming Returning Members and Members Baptized in Other Traditions" will be used. The "Welcoming" rite is intended for those who are returning after having left the church for a time and for those coming from other traditions; it would need to be adapted for those who have never left the church and who seek the rite of confirmation or reaffirmation.

Contrary to the guidance of the BOS, some parishes use only the rite of admission for all of the types of candidates, including the already-baptized candidates for confirmation/reception/reaffirmation. In such a case, care must be taken not to confuse the two groups. The language of the rite will need to be adapted—for example, the reply to the query, "What do you seek?" should be adapted to, "Deeper life in Christ," or something similar for those who seek confirmation/ reception/reaffirmation. One would not want to imply that the already-baptized do not already share in life in Christ!

After the sermon (or after the creed) the celebrant invites those to be admitted as catechumens to come forward. They stand before the congregation, facing the celebrant, with their sponsors standing behind them. A server or other assistant stands next to the celebrant, to hold the liturgical book when necessary. The celebrant then asks each person to be admitted, "What do you seek?" and each responds, "Life in Christ."

While the rubrics allow a group query and response, it is much more powerful to ask each catechumen separately. Those to be admitted will need to be coached before the service to reply in a loud voice. The sponsors stand behind them at this point because those to be admitted are expected to kneel shortly, with their sponsors' hand upon their shoulders.

When each has been queried, the celebrant recites the two great commandments and asks those to be admitted if they accept the commandments. This, and the two questions that follow (if they will be regular in worship and attending instruction, and if they will hear the Word) are asked collectively of those to be admitted, who respond as a group. The question put to the sponsors is likewise asked of the group.

The initial question and response ("What do you seek?/ Life in Christ") is sufficient individual examination. The remaining questions serve as a roadmap of the next stage in the catechumenal process and should be audible to all.

Those to be admitted kneel, if practical, while their sponsors stand behind them and place a hand on the shoulder of the one sponsored. The celebrant extends both hands over them, palms down, and prays for God's support of their intentions. A server or assistant holds the liturgical book for the celebrant.

This prayer is an important punctuation to the queries and promises that preceded it. It is very brief, but it should not be rushed.

A catechist then reads the name of each person to be admitted, and the celebrant marks the catechumen's forehead with the sign of the cross, saying the formula "N., receive the sign of the Cross on your forehead and in your heart, in the Name of the

Father, and of the Son, and of the Holy Spirit." The sponsor then silently marks the catechumen's forehead.

The signing is the final bit of business marking admission as a catechumen. The action should be as visible as possible. The space will dictate whether the celebrant moves to each kneeling catechumen, or whether the catechumens will each in turn come forward to the celebrant to receive the mark of the cross. The practice in a few places of using oil for this signing ("Oil of Catechumens") is best resisted. Anglican practice generally has only two oils in use, chrism (at baptism) and oil of the sick (at healing rites). We need not appropriate the Roman Church's third oil, and in any case no official worship book of the Episcopal Church provides a formula for consecrating such an oil.

The catechumens and sponsors then return to their places. The liturgy continues with the creed and the Prayers of the People, in the course of which prayer is offered for the new catechumens by name.

The *Book of Occasional Services* inexplicably implies that the creed might be omitted here, but this rite should always take place at a principal liturgy on a Sunday or Holy Day, which requires that the creed be said.

The prayers of the people at this liturgy and at every liturgy until the baptisms (and confirmations/receptions/reaffirmations) should include prayer, by name, for the catechumens.

WELCOMING RETURNING MEMBERS AND MEMBERS BAPTIZED IN OTHER TRADITIONS

This rite is designed for those who are going through a catechumenal process of preparation for confirmation/reception/reaffirmation. In a parish that has both catechumens (those seeking baptism) and these other sorts of candidates, it would be wise to combine both groups in the catechumenate sessions and to have this "mile-marker" rite on the same Sunday (First Sunday of Advent) as the admission of catechumens. The rubrics anticipate that this rite would take place after the prayers of the people, while the rite of admission would take place before them. That separation in time helps distinguish the catechumens (who are unbaptized) from these candidates (who are already baptized). This is not the structure that we normally use for various blessing and commissioning rites, which generally fall after the sermon and creed and before the prayers of the people, so that those who have been blessed or commissioned can be prayed for in their new capacity. It would be better to shift this rite of welcome to fall directly after the rite of admission, to preserve that structure. The suggestions below follow the pattern in the *Book of Occasional Services*, with the rite following the prayers of the people. But shifting the rite to follow immediately after the rite of admission would both mark the solidarity of all those going through the catechumenal sessions, whether "true" catechumens (the unbaptized) or candidates for confirmation/reception/reaffirmation (the baptized) and, more helpfully, solve some of the serious problems with the ending of this rite (sketched below). One might reasonably make such a shift with the permission of the bishop, as the chief liturgical officer of the diocese.

This rite omits any reference to those who have not left the church but are engaged in a catechumenal process toward confirmation or reaffirmation. It is intended for those who are returning after having left the church for a time and for those coming from other traditions. Therefore, the rite will need to be adapted for some of the likely candidates for the renewal of baptismal vows.

During the prayers of the people, those who are to be welcomed or admitted are prayed for by name. After the prayers of the people, the celebrant invites those to be welcomed to come forward. They stand before the congregation, facing the celebrant, with their sponsors standing behind them. A server or other assistant stands next to the celebrant, to hold the liturgical book when necessary.

> *A catechist presents the baptized to the celebrant with these or other words:*
> N., We present to you these persons, who are undertaking a process of growth in the meaning of their baptism.
>
> *Celebrant (to each baptized person):* What do you seek?
>
> *Answer [of those seeking reception or who have returned to the church]:* Renewal of my life in Christ.
>
> *Answer [possible alternative answer, for those seeking confirmation or reaffirmation who have never left the church]:* Deeper life in Christ.

The presentation and the initial query of the candidates need adaptation to fit those who have not left the church. The language here is permitted by the BOS rubric, which allows "these or other words." The alternative response is not, strictly speaking, necessary, as anyone might find renewal of their life in Christ a good thing, but if anyone scruples at the concept of renewing what had not grown stale, the language of deepening might serve.

The celebrant, candidates, and sponsors follow the question-and-answer dialogue in the Book of Occasional Services. *The query to the congregation is adapted:*

Celebrant (to the congregation): Will you who witness these promises keep (N., N.) in your prayers and help them, share with them your ministry, bear their burdens, and forgive and encourage them?

People: We will, with God's help.

The query is adapted to cover both those making a new beginning (by returning to the church after a time apart or by joining from another tradition) and those who are seeking confirmation or the reaffirmation of baptismal vows, but who have not left the church.

Those being presented remain standing. The sponsors, standing behind them, place a hand on their shoulders. The celebrant extends both hands over those presented, palms down, and prays for the renewal of the Holy Spirit in them.

The remaining ceremonies—writing the name in the church register of baptized persons and the welcoming (from the baptismal rite)—are unhelpful and should be omitted. Writing the name in the baptismal register would better be done after the rite of reception, if at all, because it is reception that formally recognizes the candidate as a member of the one, holy, catholic, and apostolic church and receives them into fellowship. Similarly, the welcoming is highly misleading. It appropriates language used in the baptismal rite to address the newly baptized, in the baptismal rite, and it speaks of recognizing the candidates as part of the household of God. It is the rite of reception that formally recognizes these persons, and it is baptism that makes one part of the household of God. It would be better simply to end the rite after the prayer over the candidates and then exchange the peace.

ENROLLMENT FOR LENTEN PREPARATION

According to the BOS, this rite is used at the principal service on Ash Wednesday. After the blessing of the ashes and before their imposition, the senior warden or other representative of the congregation presents the baptized to the celebrant. It is preferable that this rite instead be used at the principal eucharist on the First Sunday of Lent, after sermon and before the enrollment of candidates for baptism.

The insertion of the enrollment of candidates for confirmation/reception/ reaffirmation into Ash Wednesday is a bit out of place, because the prayer book's invitation to the observance of a holy Lent (at page 265) specifically refers to the preparation of candidates for baptism (not the renewal of baptismal vows) and to the reconciliation of penitents. It is this latter category that explains the timing: the drafting committee that produced the rites for those seeking confirmation/ reception/reaffirmation used as the basis for their work the ancient church's order of penitents and contemporary revivals of it in the Roman Catholic Church. As has been noted, this is an unhelpful linkage.

Perhaps the "mile-marker" rites could have been inverted, with the enrollment of baptismal candidates at this liturgy and the others deferred until the First Sunday of Lent—that would at least match the insertion to the language of the invitation to a holy Lent. But any insertion here is a disruption of a proper liturgy that is quite powerful in its structure, language, and imagery. The insertion of this lengthy text between the blessing of the ashes and their imposition is particularly awkward. It would be best to defer the enrollment to the First Sunday of Lent. Prudence would dictate that making such a shift would require the bishop's permission, because one would be ignoring the rubric that dictates that the rite happen at the Ash Wednesday liturgy.

The ceremonial suggestions that follow could be used regardless of the timing of the rite.

It should be noted that the term "enrollment" is a misnomer, in that the candidates are not actually enrolled—their names are not recorded as part of the rite. Instead, this rite (before 1994 termed "The Calling of the Baptized to Continuing Conversion") might better be labeled a "recognition" or even "admission." Alternatively, a book would need to be supplied to record the names of these candidates. This could be done in the same book used for baptismal

with these or other words

candidates, perhaps in a separate section, or in a separate book. Care would need to be taken, however, to ensure that the two sorts of candidates were not confused in a combined liturgy. The use of a book to enroll these candidates for confirmation/reception/reaffirmation may not be worth the potential confusion.

The candidates for confirmation/reception/reaffirmation come forward and stand facing the celebrant, with their sponsors behind them. A server or assistant stands next to the celebrant, to hold the liturgical book when necessary. A catechist presents the candidates to the celebrant with these or other words:

> N., we present to you N., N., who have been growing in an understanding of their call as Christians and are preparing to renew their baptismal covenant at Easter.

The prose of the BOS rite needs a bit of revision for stylistic reasons.

✳ *Rubrics*

The celebrant examines the candidates in their fidelity to the baptismal covenant.

The queries posed by the celebrant roughly parallel the baptismal covenant, asking about the candidates' adherence to the Christian faith and life.

After the examination, in full view of the congregation, those enrolled kneel (if practical) or bow their heads. Their sponsors stand behind them and place a hand on their shoulders. The celebrant extends both hands over the candidates, palms down, with an assistant or server holding the liturgical book. The celebrant prays for the renewal of the Holy Spirit in the candidates. The candidates stand.

If it is desired that the names of these candidates be recorded to make this an actual "enrollment," then it might be done here. A book (and stand) could be placed nearby, with the candidates each signing in turn at the conclusion of the rite. However, this risks confusing the two groups of candidates: the baptized who seek to renew their vows and the unbaptized who prepare for baptism.

If the rite takes place at the Ash Wednesday liturgy (not the recommended practice, but the one imagined by the BOS), the service continues with the imposition of ashes. If the rite takes place at the First Sunday of Lent, the service continues with these candidates returning to their places while the catechumens come forward for the enrollment of ✳ *candidates for baptism.*

ENROLLMENT OF CANDIDATES FOR BAPTISM

The enrollment of candidates for baptism takes place at the principal eucharist on the First Sunday of Lent. If the enrollment of candidates for confirmation/reception/reaffirmation takes place at the same liturgy, it happens before the enrollment of candidates for baptism.

It is recommended that the enrollment of candidates for baptism and the enrollment of candidates for confirmation/reception/reaffirmation be combined at the same liturgy. There seems very little purpose in separating the two by four days, except to underscore the difference between those who have already been baptized and those who have not. That same distinction could be preserved adequately even if both enrollments happen at the same eucharist. There are some advantages in having both sorts of candidates enrolled on the same day, as it fosters their sense of solidarity with one another. We have already noted the serious disadvantages to the insertion of the rite into the Ash Wednesday liturgy.

When the two rites of enrollment take place at the same liturgy, the candidates for confirmation/reception/reaffirmation are enrolled first, in order that the litany for the baptismal candidates might be used as the prayers of the people.

The enrollment of candidates for baptism at the Great Vigil of Easter takes place on the First Sunday in Lent. The large book in which the names of the candidates for baptism are to be written is placed where it can easily be seen and used, preferably on a portable stand or lectern that might be removed at the peace and before the offertory.

If the enrollment of candidates for confirmation/reception/reaffirmation is combined with the enrollment of candidates for baptism, it is important that the distinction between the two groups be maintained. If the choice has been made to have the former enrolled in a book, one might use a separate book or at least a separate section of the same book.

After the creed, the catechumens to be enrolled are invited to come forward with their sponsors. The catechumens stand, facing the celebrant, with their sponsors behind them. A catechist, or other lay representative of the congregation, presents them to the celebrant. The celebrant queries the sponsors collectively about the catechumens' preparation, then asks the congregation if it approves of the catechumens' enrollment as candidates for baptism.

These questions are asked of the sponsors as a group. They are not as significant as the question that follows.

The celebrant then asks each catechumen, individually, "Do you desire to be baptized?"
The individual query here mirrors that used in the rite of admission. It is also a powerful witness to the individual's will, and it serves to highlight the momentous step being taken. While it is permitted in the BOS to ask this question of all the catechumens, collectively, it is more powerful to ask it individually. (By contrast, the candidates preparing for confirmation/reception/reaffirmation are asked their questions collectively.)

The celebrant formally accepts the catechumens as candidates for baptism. A catechist reads each candidate's name aloud as the candidate writes her name in the book.
This is the actual "enrollment," and as such it is the action at the heart of the rite. It should not be minimized, nor passed over quickly in the name of "efficiency."

The candidates remain together at the front of the church while the deacon or a catechist leads the litany. After the petition for the families and friends of the baptismal candidates, the following is inserted:

> For those who will solemnly renew their baptismal covenant at Easter, let us pray to the Lord.
>
> *Lord, have mercy.*

The celebrant extends both hands, palms down, and says the concluding prayer over the candidates for baptism. A server or assistant holds the liturgical book for the celebrant.
The candidates then return to their places and the liturgy continues with the confession of sin (or with the peace, if the penitential order was used at the start of the liturgy).
Beginning at this eucharist, the candidates for baptism should be prayed for by name at every eucharist in Lent. When Eucharistic Prayer D is used, they should be included by name in the "diptychs" on page 375, with "Remember all your people, and those who seek your truth."
"Remember N., N., and N., who prepare for baptism at the Great Vigil of Easter." One might also include other candidates, with an additional petition

following: "Remember N. and N. who will renew their baptismal vows." If Eucharistic Prayer D is not used, the candidates for baptism (and candidates for confirmation/reception/reaffirmation) should be included in the prayers of the people.

RITES DURING CANDIDACY FOR BAPTISM

The *Book of Occasional Services* offers several prayers and blessings that may be used for the baptismal candidates during Lent. It is suggested that these be used on the Third, Fourth, and Fifth Sundays of Lent. Conveniently, three prayers and three blessings are provided, one pairing for each Sunday. These prayers and blessings are a version of the sixth-century Lenten scrutinies of the candidates, which took place on these Sundays and which have been revived in RCIA. In their original form, each scrutiny was an examination and exorcism of the candidate; the RCIA version preserves this character while the BOS has moderated it quite a bit.

Additionally, the BOS suggests that the Apostles' Creed be given to the candidates on the Third Sunday of Lent, and the Lord's Prayer on the Fifth Sunday of Lent, following the prayers. These prayers and rituals are not as significant as the rite of admission or the rite of enrollment, and they could be omitted without significant loss.

These prayers (and the giving of the creed and Lord's Prayer that may follow) are inserted directly before the prayers of the people.

After the sermon (and creed, unless it is to be given as part of the rite), the celebrant invites the candidates for baptism and their sponsors to come forward and stand before the congregation. A server or assistant stands next to the celebrant to hold the liturgical book. The candidates face the celebrant and kneel or bow their heads, with the sponsors standing behind them. The sponsors each place a hand on their candidate's shoulder. The celebrant invites the congregation to silent prayer. After a substantial period of silence, the celebrant extends both hands, palms down, over the candidates and says one of the indicated prayers. The celebrant then goes to each candidate in turn and lays hands on her head in silence, praying silently for a period of time. The celebrant returns to her original position, facing the group, and says the indicated blessing. The candidates and sponsors return to their places, and the liturgy continues with the prayers of the people.

This rite is full of silence, which should not be rushed. The entire assembly prays silently for the candidates before the celebrant offers a concluding collect, to terminate the period of prayer. This is followed by the imposition of hands with more silent prayer, during which the congregation should be praying silently as well. The final blessing is really a dismissal of the candidates back to their places. (In parishes that practice the dismissal of catechumens, it would happen at this point.)

If the creed is to be given, the normal recitation of the Nicene Creed directly after the sermon is omitted. After the blessing of the candidates by the celebrant, a catechist introduces the congregation's recitation of the creed. The celebrant and people say the creed together, all standing. Either the Apostles' Creed or the Nicene Creed may be used, but the Apostles' Creed is to be preferred. After the creed, the celebrant concludes the recitation, and the candidates and sponsors return to their places (or are dismissed).

The "giving" of the creed is really its recitation by the congregation. A duplication of the creed is avoided, so the recitation that would normally follow immediately after the sermon and before the prayers for the candidates is omitted, and the only recitation is in the giving of the creed. While the Nicene Creed is the customary creed at the eucharist, the Apostles' Creed is the baptismal creed and the one that the candidate will recite at the Easter Vigil. For this reason, it is recommended to use the Apostles' Creed here.

If the Lord's Prayer is to be given (on the Fifth Sunday of Lent), the candidates bow their heads and the sponsors place a hand on their shoulders. A catechist introduces the giving of the prayer with the words, "Let the candidates for baptism now receive the Lord's Prayer from the church." The celebrant then invites the congregation to join in the prayer, using the customary introduction from the eucharist ("As our Savior Christ has taught us . . ."). The congregation recites the prayer, after which the celebrant adds the concluding sentence (and dismissal, in those places where it is practiced): "May the Lord remain with you." The candidates and sponsors return to their places (or depart, if dismissed).

The "giving" of the Lord's Prayer is its recitation by the congregation. Because the ordinary recitation after the eucharistic prayer is distant in time, there is no reason to be concerned about the duplication here; in places where the catechumens are dismissed, they would not hear the recapitulation, in any case. It would seem harmless for the catechist to give both the introduction ("Let the candidates . . .") and the invitation to the congregation ("As our Savior Christ has taught us . . ."), except that the celebrant is the normative presider in the community's worship, and this prayer is part of the worship of the church.

MAUNDY THURSDAY RITE OF PREPARATION FOR THE PASCHAL HOLY DAYS

This rite, intended for baptized candidates for confirmation/reception/reaffirmation, is well intentioned, but it is of very limited practical use. It is based on an ancient form of the solemn reconciliation of penitents, but the penitential tone that survives poses difficulties for its use for most of these candidates in the present day, as they are not necessarily penitents.

It might possibly make sense to use this rite in the case of those who had left the church for a time, of their own volition, and now have returned to seek the rite of reaffirmation. But even here, the rite of preparation poses difficulties: those returning to the church, if the BOS sequence has been followed, have already been welcomed back to the fellowship of the church in the rite of "Welcoming Returning Members and Members Baptized in Other Traditions." Presumably they have shared in the eucharist since at least that point. Additionally, while someone's voluntary departure from the church may indicate separation from the congregation, it does not necessarily mean that the one who left was guilty of sin. The ancient rite for the solemn reconciliation of penitents, on which this rite of preparation was based at least in part, was really about restoring to the church's fellowship (eucharistic and otherwise) those who had been excluded by sin, expelled from the church as a penalty, and then undergone rigorous penance. The rite of public reconciliation of penitents was the last stage in a separation that the church itself imposed. Those returning to the church in the present day, by contrast, have left and returned of their own accord, without being ejected by the church. Thus, the rite of preparation is based on an inapplicable model.

The rite of preparation strikes an unhelpful note, both theologically and pastorally. Candidates for confirmation/reception/reaffirmation are not penitents, and they have not been excluded from the sacramental life of the church (the latter fact being part of the reason that the BOS takes such pains to distinguish them from the "true" catechumens, who are unbaptized and therefore do not share in the eucharist). From the standpoint of ecumenism and pastoral common sense, it makes little sense to send the explicit message to those coming into the church from a different tradition, through the rite of reception, that their prior church affiliation is cause to do penance. It makes just as little sense to tell those who have never left the church and now seek confirmation or to reaffirm their vows to do public penance. The Maundy Thursday rite of preparation is best avoided.

The only circumstance in which it would make theological, pastoral, and liturgical sense would be if someone had been publicly repelled from communion, under the disciplinary rubrics (the only basis, in the Episcopal Church, for barring a penitent from communion). In that case, one might conceivably use this rite, with the penitent's agreement and after individual confession using the prayer book forms for reconciliation of a penitent. The restored penitent might then reaffirm baptismal vows at the next visit by the bishop. One can barely imagine the circumstances in which such a ritual process, being so public, would be pastorally appropriate and would be consented to by the penitent.

CONCLUSION

The rites of Christian initiation require preparation, and the catechumenate offers the best approach available for the formation of candidates for baptism, confirmation, reception, and the reaffirmation of baptism. While the *Book of Occasional Services* supplies outlines of three processes and several rites, a good bit of local adaptation is required. The outlines are simply that, and so the clergy and lay leaders will need to decide what content to bring to the catechumenal processes, as well as the details of the structure. The rites for the "true" catechumens (the unbaptized) are effective, but those for the baptized who seek confirmation/reception/reaffirmation require sub-stantial adaptation. One might hope that in future revisions of the *Book of Occasional Services*, these rites leading to the renewal of baptismal vows might be addressed.

The catechumenate (and its parallel processes for the baptized) therefore requires quite a bit of work on the part of a parish's leadership before it can be implemented. One would be well advised to start planning about a year before launching the process in a parish, as it will take nearly that long to enlist the parish leadership, develop the content to be addressed, and identify and train catechists. The catechumenate tends to become one of the central aspects of a community's life, both because of the high degree of energy and investment required and because of the significant, positive impact it can have on the faith and commitment of those who go through it. It is not, therefore, just another program to be added to the slate of parish programs. It is at once both more demanding and more life-giving.

Notes

1. Johnson, *Rites of Christian Initiation*, 33–88, 301–2.

2. Bradshaw, Johnson, and Phillips, eds., *Apostolic Tradition*, 82–125.

3. Johnson, *Rites of Christian Initiation*, 33–88, 301–2.

4. *RCIA*, 5

5. BOS, 114–15.

6. [Episcopal Church], *The Book of Occasional Services* (New York: Church Publishing, 1979), 114; [Episcopal Church], *The Book of Occasional Services: Conforming to the General Convention, 1988* (New York: Church Hymnal Corporation, 1988), 114; [Episcopal Church], *The Book of Occasional Services, 1991: Conforming to General Convention 1991* (New York: Church Hymnal Corporation, 1991), 114; [Episcopal Church], *The Book of Occasional Services, 1994: Conforming to General Convention 1994* (New York: Oxford University Press, 1995), 116; Johnson, *Rites of Christian Initiation*, 332–33; Meyers, *Continuing the Reformation*, 217.

7. Kavanagh, *Shape of Baptism*, 108.

8. Kavanagh, *Shape of Baptism*, 110.

9. BOS, 161.

10. BOS, 159–61.

11. BOS, 161.

12. BCP 1979, 298; BOS, 114, 137, 159–61.

13. BCP 1979, 302.

14. Robert Brooks, correspondence with author, August 24, 2012.

Chapter 4

PERFORMANCE NOTES

Liturgy, at its basic roots, is performative, not unlike a play. The play is much more than the words prescribed in the script; it is also the staging, action, props, set, and the way the lines are delivered. In the same way, the liturgy is more than just the words in the Book of Common Prayer. The liturgy has its staging and action—the movements and gestures in the act of worship. The liturgy also has its set-dressing, props, and costumes. While the liturgy is deeper in its meaning and implications, nevertheless good liturgical practitioners must be aware of some of the same performative elements with which theatrical directors and actors are concerned.

The performance of the liturgy can assist in bringing out its meaning and in facilitating the participation of the assembly; it can undercut the theology of the rite and short-circuit the meaningful participation of the faithful; or it can simply desiccate the rite, sucking the life out of it. Baptism and the rites of confirmation/reception/reaffirmation must be carefully prepared and performed, or we can inadvertently undermine the liturgy.

RITUAL PREPARATION

Preparation for a ritual involves more than just the readying of a space and props. It extends to the preparation of candidates over the months and weeks prior to the day when they will make or renew their baptismal vows. It also entails the ritual formation of a congregation, so that it is ready to engage in the liturgy as active participants. It requires considerable reflection and planning, as well as rehearsal.

In good ritual preparation, the presider and her or his assistants (clergy and lay) will make careful, intentional choices about all of the elements of the liturgy. They will also rehearse all of the participants in their roles before the actual baptisms and confirmations.

Careful liturgical planning needs to involve, at a minimum, the presider; the priest in charge the parish, if that is a different person; the parish musician or music director; the person who creates the bulletins or service booklets; and the person or persons who coordinate the lay volunteers who serve in the liturgy and arrange the liturgical space for use. These participants should meet well in advance of the liturgy being planned, particularly in the case of such complex events as the Great Vigil of Easter. This group should debrief the last time the liturgy took place (for example, the last baptism or the last Easter Vigil), noting what worked well and what did not. Then the group should begin to prepare the upcoming liturgy, with attention to the options in liturgical text, music, and choreography, and to the constraints of the space and personnel available. Subsequently, the planning group should touch base as the date of the liturgy approaches, to ensure that necessary preparations are well under way. The week of the liturgy, planners should touch base again, and after the liturgy it is important to have a meeting to discuss what worked and what did not, with an eye toward keeping that information, as well as any planning aids and the service booklet, on file as a reference for the next time.

The exception to this general rule is a liturgy at which the bishop presides. In this case, the presider (the bishop) will rarely be able to meet in person with the other liturgical planners. Under these circumstances, it generally works best for the priest in charge of the parish to send a draft of the liturgy at least eight weeks in advance to the bishop, along with a letter outlining ritual needs and any unusual parish customs. The bishop may then revise the draft and return it for further work.

Liturgical planners are not the only ones who must prepare. Candidates and sponsors need to be prepared to take part in their roles, as do clergy and lay assistants. It is important to rehearse all participants in the liturgy. To quote Robert Hovda, "to assume that the Holy Spirit assists only the unprepared is to give insufficient glory to God."[1] Rehearsal accomplishes three goals. First, the liturgy unfolds with less disruption when participants know what they are doing. Second, for ritual to be effective, it needs to be unself-conscious, and rehearsal can help achieve that. Third, participants need to have a sense of occasion, and rehearsal can help them acquire that.

The liturgy works better when participants know what they are doing. As obvious as this may seem, it is too often ignored, with the clergy giving audible stage directions throughout the liturgy, because they had not bothered to rehearse candidates and sponsors. Oral directions—even just the giving of page numbers—tend to yank participants out of the moment and disrupt the occasion. That is bad enough on a normal Sunday, but it is worse in the midst of the rites of initiation.

For ritual to do its work, participants must not be self-conscious. While ritual is patterned symbolic behavior, and therefore scripted, nevertheless participants must enter into the liturgical act with abandon. They need to be immersed in the experience. Preparation is needed to accomplish this: one must rehearse the liturgy with candidates and sponsors in particular until they are reasonably familiar with their parts (and until the presider is comfortable that they will do them!). Liturgical assistants need to be rehearsed as well, unless they are so familiar with their roles that they can move through them as if by second nature. Even then, rehearsal is beneficial.

Finally, ritual participants also need to have a sense of the occasion. Rehearsal can help in this by explaining in age-appropriate terms what will happen and something of its meaning. Candidates and sponsors need to understand baptism as "spine-chilling rites of initiation."[2] This is not to say that children need to be suppressed or adults scared senseless, or to deny that what is age-appropriate will vary widely from toddler to elderly person, but candidates need to have some sense of the awesome nature of what they are doing. This will enable them to enter into the initiatory act with a dose of holy awe as well as joy. A separate session talking through the text of the rite, allowing for questions and discussion on the part of older children and adults, is a good addition prior to the actual rehearsal of stage directions and movements.

This specific preparation for the rites of initiation should be just one part of the overall ritual formation of the people of God. Persons of all ages, including small children, should be present in the liturgy, regularly participating in an age-appropriate fashion. Catechumens were historically dismissed before the liturgy of the table, and it is permitted to do so now, but an opportunity for learning by observation will be missed. Certainly, the baptized, including the smallest children, should be present for the whole of the eucharist. Fears that children will be disruptive are often misplaced. Soft toys, crayons and paper, and other quiet diversions can help children during a sermon aimed at adults, and the rest of the liturgy should be sufficiently engaging to hold their attention for at least part of the time. Singing the hymns, listening to the stories embedded in scriptural texts, and watching the liturgical action of the eucharistic prayer and distribution all provide moments that parents can use to involve and form their children. Parents often find that sitting in the front of the church, rather than the back, helps children engage in the liturgy. Offering Sunday school lessons or "children's chapel" in a separate space during the parish eucharist is an insult to the bonds of baptism, not to mention counterproductive. Being present for the liturgy—all of it—and participating in age-appropriate ways help form children for worship.

SCHEDULING

The priest in charge of a parish can do a great deal to help or hinder the rites of initiation by deciding when those rites will be scheduled. The 1979 BCP is quite clear: the normal rite of baptism (as opposed to emergency baptisms *in extremis*) can only be scheduled on a Sunday or other major feast, at the principal eucharist of the day. Private baptism is a grave error, because baptism is public business at its heart: bringing the individual into new relationship with God through Christ and with the body of Christ, accepting the shared responsibilities of life in the community of the faithful (as represented in the baptismal covenant). Further, the prayer book is clear that baptisms should be restricted, so far as possible, to four calendrical occasions plus the bishop's visit. The calendrical occasions are not arbitrary: Easter Vigil, the Day of Pentecost, the Feast of the Baptism of Our Lord, and All Saints' Day or the Sunday following.[3] Each has a particular resonance that fits the church's baptismal theology, and the lectionary readings assigned to each day support the weight of the occasion.

The Easter Vigil was, at least in some early Christian communities, the paramount occasion for baptisms. Tertullian cited it in the beginning of the third century as the preferred date of baptism. By the fourth century Easter and Pentecost were the sole occasions for baptism in Rome, and Easter was the only permissible occasion in Milan.[4] The emphasis on the Vigil as the baptismal feast persisted in Rome long after the shift to the normative baptism of infants.[5]

More important than historical precedent alone, the occasion of the Great Vigil lends itself to baptism. The Vigil stresses the theme of the Lord's resurrection, into which we are baptized, and it embeds the newly baptized in the entire narrative of salvation history. The opening address at the kindling of the new fire and the Exsultet that follows both frame the Vigil as *anamnesis*—that sort of rich remembering that calls a past event into the present and makes it real for the participants. The lessons from the Hebrew scripture that follow set forth an abbreviated narrative of salvation history, culminating in the baptismal rite. In the first eucharist of Easter that follows, participants hear the narrative of Jesus' resurrection from Matthew's gospel, as well as Paul's commentary in Romans. Finally, in the eucharistic prayer there is another *anamnesis* of the resurrection and its efficacy for us. The Vigil is shot through with baptismal themes, in its natural emphasis on the resurrection of Jesus Christ and its assertion that through our worship we participate in this paschal mystery.

Baptism is such an integral part of the Easter Vigil that in the absence of candidates for initiation, the prayer book requires the use of the form for renewal of baptismal vows. On its own, this renewal of vows connects the congregation to the baptismal themes of the liturgy, though without much of the symbolic force of an actual baptism. In some parishes, it is also the custom to bless the water in the font with the recitation of the full Thanksgiving over the Water and to sprinkle the assembly, in the asperges. This expansion of the prayer book's provisions for the Vigil without candidates is a reasonable way to deal with the ritual impoverishment of a baptism-less rite, but it is not as powerful as the full Vigil, with baptisms. The ritual force of the thing would be enough, to my mind, to reserve baptisms strictly to the Vigil and the bishop's visit. The Vigil readings appropriately support the baptismal occasion, and conversely the absence of a baptism weakens the experience of the Vigil. Yet in too many places, baptisms are conducted not at the Vigil but at the late morning eucharist on Easter Sunday. This weakens the Vigil and deprives the baptismal liturgy of its proper setting. Easter morning's eucharist is, after all, simply one Sunday eucharist in the Great Fifty Days of Easter.

Finally, the Easter Vigil is really the only appropriate time, apart from the bishop's visit, for the baptism of adult candidates if the catechumenate has been used to prepare them. While the *Book of Occasional Services* offers the alternative schedule of a catechumenal process culminating at the Feast of the Baptism of Our Lord, its clearly stated preference is to restrict the baptism of adult catechumens to the Great Vigil of Easter. The catechumenate does not work well if a baptismal date other than the Vigil is used.[6] The catechumenate involves stages that are linked to the church calendar, and those stages (and their milepost rituals) do not make as much sense apart from their calendrical seasons. The final period of "Candidacy" and preparation for baptism, for example, fits best with the season of Lent, whose historical origins had much to do with baptismal preparation.[7]

The Day of Pentecost has its own resonance with baptismal themes. In baptism, the candidate receives the gift of the Holy Spirit; the Day of Pentecost celebrates the coming of the Holy Spirit to the Church as a whole. Baptism on the Day of Pentecost underscores the pneumatic element in Christian initiation. It is also in keeping with ample historical precedent in the early church.[8]

A third baptismal occasion in the 1979 prayer book, the Feast of the Baptism of our Lord, falls on the first Sunday after the Epiphany. It lacks the pneumatological content of Pentecost or the resurrection theme of Easter, but it is the commemoration of Jesus' own baptism. Because his baptism is the warrant for the practice of his followers, it is a most fitting occasion for baptism. Homiletically, it offers a clear link between the action of Jesus at the river Jordan and the action of the church and the new initiate today. Baptism on this feast also has deep, historical roots, particularly in the East. For example, Gregory of Nazianzus testified in one of his *Theological Orations* that Epiphany baptism was customary, while it also took place in Syria and Spain.[9]

The final calendrical occasion is All Saints' Day or the Sunday following (if the feast is transferred, as the prayer book allows). This does not have historical grounding as a baptismal occasion, but there is a certain homiletical advantage to a day that celebrates the communion of saints, which one joins in one's baptism, a point made by Boone Porter when he first proposed it. There are also some practical advantages: a baptismal date in the fall spaces the calendrical opportunities more evenly, allowing baptism between Pentecost and Epiphany.[10]

On each of these occasions, the baptismal rite and the calendrical themes reinforce each other. For this reason, the Easter Vigil requires the use of the Renewal of Baptismal Vows when there are no candidates for baptism, while for the other feasts the prayer book encourages the substitution of the Renewal of Baptismal Vows in place of the Nicene Creed. This substitution is a useful one in any community that does not have candidates for baptism on a regular basis, because it reinforces the church's core theology, implanting the baptismal covenant in the consciousness of each believer.

The final occasion specified for baptism is the bishop's visit to a parish. The bishop is the chief minister of the sacraments, including Christian initiation. By presiding in the baptismal rite in the midst of the gathered community, with the deacons and presbyters of that community assisting, the bishop offers an image of the liturgy in its most complete form. Subsequent baptisms performed by a presbyter then can be seen for what they are: the bishop's delegate operating on behalf of the absent bishop. Encouraging baptism when the bishop visits also allows adult candidates (and the parish) to experience full Christian initiation in the baptismal rite, without the confusion posed by subsequent confirmation. The candidate receives the imposition of the hand and chrismation from the bishop after the administration of the water, and the prayer book is clear that subsequent confirmation is unnecessary, redundant, and misleading.[11]

Baptism is not about a baby having its special day; it is about our shared discipleship as we follow Jesus. This is a hard saying, and one that has not been received in all places, but it is crucial to appropriate baptismal practice, with implications for choices about the staging and conduct of the liturgy. Baptism is about being grafted into the body of Christ, and so it is at root a corporate act grounded in a common mission, not one child's special day or one family's celebration. Following the calendrical wisdom of the BCP and limiting baptism to the four specified dates plus the bishop's visit has the effect of massing multiple baptisms together in mid- to large-size congregations, undermining attempts to emphasize an individual's specialness. Good ritual procedure must also be used within the rite, of course, and some often-observed practices will need to be avoided (discussed below). But sticking to the calendrical rules can greatly help in making the point—integral to the church's baptismal theology—that baptism is about our corporate life as a church and the individual's new place in the body of Christ. Absent a truly life-threatening emergency, there is no reason why baptisms cannot be reserved to these four calendrical occasions plus the bishop's visit. Baptisms should not be scheduled outside those times.

Sign-value

Liturgics scholars and good liturgical practitioners often speak of the "sign-value" of a liturgical element. It is a way of describing the efficacy or potency of signs and symbols, their ability to communicate. Much of the energy of liturgical practitioners from the second half of the twentieth century onward has been put into the effort to reinvigorate the central symbols of the Christian liturgy.[12] To speak of a liturgical element as having greater "sign-value" is to say that it communicates its meaning with clarity, integrity, and vigor.

Liturgical texts matter, of course, but even the best words can be undermined by the physical stuff of the liturgy and the way it is used. And sometimes both physical gesture and the material objects of the liturgy speak their symbolic meaning more effectively without words at all. As Robert Hovda put it aptly, "The sacraments cause because they signify, and therefore they depend as much upon the communicative power of symbol and gesture as they do upon that of the word. . . ."[13] The overuse of words can trample gestures and symbols that are far more effective on their own. More frequently, the physical stuff of the liturgy is not used in a way that inspires one to take its symbolic meaning seriously. Anglicanism has always had a particular emphasis on the Incarnation, and we are a church that uses lots of stuff: bread, wine, oil, water, incense. The enfleshment of our signs and symbols should be given careful attention. To call the eucharist a feast of bread and wine, even an anticipation of the messianic banquet, and then to pass out prefabricated disks or pasteurized grape juice in individual shot glasses is to undercut the liturgy through the deployment of weak signs.

When it comes to the baptismal rite, the issue of sign-value is chiefly one of the quantity of stuff used. Baptism is evocative of drowning: Paul wrote of one being buried with Christ, while others wrote of going down into the waters of baptism and being raised up as a new person. It is hard to make this symbol sing if one is using a salad bowl. This argues for the use of immersion, rather than pouring or sprinkling, in baptizing candidates. It is the most ancient way of baptizing, and it is also the most symbolically effective. Immersion, it should be noted, is not the same as submersion—the latter meaning that the candidate is entirely under the surface of the water. In immersion, the candidate stands or kneels in the water while water is poured over her head.

Immersing an infant requires only an ample font. The priest administering the water rolls up her alb sleeves, takes the baby in her arms, supporting the head and neck with one forearm, and simply lowers the child into the font, being careful not to submerge the mouth and nose. Alternatively, one could sit the infant in the font and pour water over the head, much like at bath time. The Eastern churches continue the early church's tradition of baptizing naked infants, and some in the West argue in favor of the practice. Parents, especially those of male children, would be understandably wary of what might ensue when certain parts are exposed to open air and then to water, notwithstanding the reassurance that urine is said to be a sterile bodily fluid. Waterproof "swimmy" diapers are a better option, as they solve the obvious problem as well as allowing the infant a bit of modesty (important to the parents, if not to an infant). After the administration of the water, the infant is lifted out of the font and given to a parent, who wraps the child in a dry towel. At the peace in the ordinary baptismal rite, or before the Easter acclamation at the Vigil, the child can be taken behind a screen or into the sacristy (or some other room) to change into dry clothes.

Immersing an adult requires a baptismal pool, either permanent or temporary. Many newer churches are built with baptismal pools, sometimes in combination with standing fonts, to allow easy immersion of both infants and adults. Temporary fonts can be constructed from wood and plastic liner material, or all manner of temporary field expedients, such as cattle troughs, can be used. To immerse an adult, the priest administering the water can enter into the pool with the candidate or can crouch alongside the pool. If the priest enters the pool, he will want to remove shoes and possibly roll up pant legs and shirt sleeves under the alb. The candidate should wear an alb or some other robe, preferably over a swimsuit or over clothes that can get wet, and should also remove shoes. The candidate kneels in the pool and bends down into the water, or kneels in the water as the priest pours water over her. At the peace in the ordinary baptismal rite, or before the Easter acclamation at the Vigil, the candidate would need to change into dry clothes. The priest would need to do the same if he had entered the water with the candidate.

If one cannot, for reasons of architecture, manage to immerse the candidate, water at least should be poured in great quantity over the candidate at the font. In the small town where I grew up, the parish used a brass bowl, no larger than a salad bowl, as the baptismal font. But because it was inconvenient to clean and polish this bowl, there was placed within it a Pyrex custard cup, about two ounces in capacity. The custard cup held the water to be used in baptism. This was such seriously impoverished symbolism as to render the deep language of the baptismal rite ludicrous. Perhaps the best guide to assessing one's container is to call to mind the extravagant imagery of the Thanksgiving over the Water before selecting the vessel. If the vessel under consideration makes one snicker as one describes its contents as the waters of creation and as the Red Sea's tides, then one needs a bigger vessel.

Once a decent font has been procured, there is still the problem of how the water within it is to be used. While it is technically true that one can indeed drown in a very small quantity of water, the sign-value of water is greater when it is poured with great abundance and flung with reckless abandon.

The water should be poured over the candidate using a pitcher or flagon, never a shell. The shell as a symbol of baptism dates from at least the Middle Ages, but its use in the administration of water has the effect of drastically limiting the sign-value of the pouring. It is simply not possible to use enough water in baptism if one uses a shell. Still worse is the practice of using a fake shell made from pottery or some metal, which contributes to the domestication of a sacrament. Baptism is about a metaphorical drowning of the old Adam, and anything that contributes to the sentimentalizing of the rite should be resisted.

After the candidates have been baptized, it is appropriate to asperge the congregation as the baptismal party returns from the font. This is a way of symbolically enacting the renewal of the baptismal covenant in which everyone in the congregation has just joined, alongside the candidates. The priest or bishop can scoop some water out of the font in a vessel and use a sprig of evergreen to sprinkle the crowd. Some church-goods merchants sell holy water sprinklers that resemble corn brooms; these are far preferable to the metal sprinklers that one can find. The other material element used in the baptismal rite is chrism. Chrism is olive oil mixed with scented oil of some kind. There are several varieties of "chrism essence" commercially available, and some recipes to "home-cook" chrism using oil of balsam. One should use good-quality oil—extra virgin oil is far more fragrant than some of the other grades, which may use heat or chemicals to maximize the extraction of oil. Holy oils are meant to reach not just the tactile but also the olfactory sense, so the extra cost of extra virgin oil is worth it.

It can be significant to consecrate chrism in full view of the parish congregation, in the course of the baptismal rite when the bishop is present, and for that chrism to be used until the bishop's next visit to the parish. This seems to be the intention of the drafters of the 1979 BCP.[14] Though the prayer book does not anticipate the consecration of chrism outside the baptismal liturgy, a form to consecrate chrism apart from baptism was included in the *Book of Occasional Services*, with a rubric indicating that it was for use "when, because of the absence of candidates for Baptism, the consecration of Chrism takes place at the time of Confirmation . . . or at some other time."[15] The rubric does not appear to anticipate large, annual diocesan events for the consecration of chrism, although it certainly does not prohibit them. The positive value of a diocesan "chrism mass" is that it allows the diocese (clergy and laity) an occasion to reflect on formation and ministry. The positive value of consecrating chrism at the bishop's visitation is that it increases the visibility of the consecration to ordinary parishioners. Generally speaking, these matters will be decided by bishops: if there is no diocesan "chrism mass," then chrism would be consecrated at visitations.

It should be noted—because one hears of occasional confusion—that chrism is quite different from the "Oil of the Sick" used in the prayer book rites for anointing those who are ill. The Oil of the Sick is typically pure, unscented olive oil, and it may be consecrated by any priest. It is often held in containers marked "OI" for *oleum infirmorum*, its Latin name; chrism containers would be marked "SC" for *sanctum chrisma*. When one encounters a container designed for the oil of catechumens—an oil not generally used in the Episcopal versions of the catechumenate—it is marked "OC" (or in very old oil stocks, "OS"). One does well to keep the oils, and their uses, distinct.

However it is procured or consecrated, the chrism should be used with the same attention to the principle of sign-value that was paid in the administration of water. Too many clergy adopt a sort of minimalist approach to the use of chrism, using oil stocks the size of thimbles containing small cotton balls that at one point had been dabbed with oil. Sometimes a great deal of time has passed since the cotton was dampened with chrism, with the result that the contents no longer resemble oil. It is best to hold the chrism in much larger containers, scaled to the space. In a small to mid-sized church, sixteen-ounce containers would be fitting, but in a larger space even they might seem puny. The containers should be made of glass, so that all may see the contents.

Then, when the bishop or priest anoints the newly baptized, she or he should use chrism in abundance. The presider may pour chrism directly onto the head of the neophyte and then trace a cross in the oil. Alternatively, the presider may pour chrism into her cupped hand, then smear it on the forehead of the neophyte and trace a cross in the oil. Chrism is a symbol the baptized share in the royal priesthood of Christ, by virtue of now being part the body of Christ. It is too significant to omit it or to use it halfheartedly. The Reformation's sacramental minimalism is now generally accepted as unhelpful, so we might reasonably come to accept chrismation as an integral part of the baptismal rite in its symbolic fullness. Baptism without chrism is of course "valid," to use loaded terminology from a Roman Catholic theological system, but chrism normatively belongs in baptism.

Good sign-value can help fight the tendency to sentimentalize the occasion. The eucharist has the advantage of not normally being associated with infancy in the popular imagination. By contrast, the most prevalent baptismal candidate in the Episcopal Church is a baby. Thus, baptism threatens to bring out every temptation to oversentimentalize what is supposed to be a life-and-death sacrament. By evoking the older, biblical image of drowning and being raised for death, good sign-value can reorient baptism away from all its misty-eyed baggage and toward its real meaning, as the sacrament by which one puts to death an old way of life and embraces a radical and demanding path of discipleship.

Fussing over everyone

It is important that we make *at least* as much fuss over adult candidates as infants. Bluntly, infants are delightful, wonderful creatures, and most of us will gush all over them, for sound evolutionary reasons. But in Christian initiation, we do well to remember that adult baptism is the liturgical norm—that which gives shape and meaning to the rite—in the Episcopal Church. Infant baptism, however lovely, is a departure from that norm.

Adult candidates very often have had to make hard choices to bring themselves to the font. The culture no longer pressures one to join a church; indeed, much of the culture looks down on the sort of forthright assertion of religious belief that an adult candidate makes. Further, many of them have had to press forward to the font in the face of discouragement or full-bore opposition from friends and family. This sort of persistence is a powerful example (and spur to reflection) for those witnessing the baptism. Infant baptismal candidates need to be celebrated, of course, but adult candidates need at least as much attention. The point is that *all* new Christians, regardless of age, should command our awe, affection, and admiration. Not all parishes do as good a job celebrating adult neophytes as they do the infants.

The place where this is often seen is at the welcoming of the newly baptized, after the water bath, consignation, and chrismation. The presider invites the assembly, "Let us welcome the newly baptized," and this is very often accompanied by the presider parading an infant neophyte up and down the aisle of the church. One very rarely, if ever, observes the presider leading an adult neophyte by the hand up and down the aisles. The parading of infants looks very much like privileging them before the newly baptized adults, and that does not square with our baptismal theology. The motive seems to be the priest's desire to be seen with the baby—as Paul Marshall has described it, the equivalent of a baby-kissing politician, bent on showing "how loving and caring the celebrant is."[16] We should not make more of a fuss over infants than we do over adults in the baptismal rite. Baptism is for all God's children, but it is not child's play—it is serious business.

When the rites of confirmation, reception, and reaffirmation take place in the baptismal rite, great care needs to be taken in their staging so that they do not overshadow baptism. They are clearly subordinate in the prayer book's text and in its theology, and so they should be subordinate in their staging and execution. Candidates for these rites should be presented after the baptismal candidates. They should join audibly in the recitation of the baptismal covenant. The newly confirmed should receive communion after the newly baptized.

CEREMONIAL COMMENTARY ON THE BAPTISMAL RITE

Let us now turn to a play-by-play description of ceremonies to accompany the baptismal rite. It should go without saying that this is simply one version of how to conduct the liturgy of baptism. It is helpful to remember the dictum, "The building always wins."[17] For a detailed guide to the celebration of the eucharist that follows the peace, one should consult Patrick Malloy, *Celebrating the Eucharist*, which is indispensable.

What follows can be easily adapted when the baptism takes place in the context of the Easter Vigil. Stage directions are given in *italicized* type; the roman type that follows such directions gives commentary and amplification.

Furniture

Baptism requires water. To be effective from a ritual standpoint, there must be water in abundance. This argues against the use of basins or bowls, and in favor of the use of fonts or pools. Often, older fonts designed strictly for infant baptism can be adapted into new forms, so that the water spills down from the old font into an immersion pool. If it is not possible to install an immersion pool in an older building, new fonts should be built large enough to allow the immersion of babies, even if one still pours water over adult candidates.

The water, whether in a pool or a font, must be located so that the congregation can observe the baptismal action. While in the early church the actual water bath took place in separate baptisteries, apart from the congregation, this was likely because of the practice of baptizing naked adults. The rest of the baptismal rite took place in full view of the congregation. Baptism is public business, so the action needs to be visible.

The font or pool should be located near the main entrance to the church, preferably on an axis with the altar, to symbolize baptism as the means of entry into the Christian community. As Aidan Kavanagh has reminded us, there are two liturgical foci in a church building: the altar and the font.[18] Every other piece of furniture, even the lectern and pulpit, is subordinate to these two, which anchor the liturgical space. One begins one's Christian life in baptism, and one renews that initiation each time one participates in the eucharist, so the spatial progression from font to altar is significant. Fonts should not be placed adjacent to altars; the two foci should not compete visually with each other.

The font or pool should be impressive in size. It must be clear that it is designed for the bathing of humans, not birds. Baptism is of equal importance with the eucharist, and so the font or pool should be at least as impressive as its altar.

There should be sufficient space around the font or pool for the ministers, candidates, and sponsors to gather for the water bath. This may require the permanent removal of some chairs or pews. The font or pool could be located in the narthex or foyer of the church, in a two-room arrangement, provided that there is sufficient space for the entire congregation to gather around the font (in which case they would join in the procession to the font, along with the candidates and sponsors, at the appropriate point in the liturgy). Few existing buildings will have that kind of gathering space, though it might be considered in new construction. In most circumstances, the font will be placed at the end of the nave near the entrance, surrounded by adequate open space, with the altar at the other end. In this configuration, the font and its surroundings become a transitional space as one moves from the narthex into the worship space of the assembly.

Vesture

Clergy and lay assistants vest, from the beginning of the liturgy, as they would for the eucharist: alb, with stole for the clergy and chasuble for the presider. A deacon may wear a dalmatic. There is no practical advantage to the use of a cope during the administration of water, and because it is a processional garment and not a presidential one, it is out of place on the celebrant at baptism. Because the baptismal liturgy is a liturgical unity, one does not change vesture partway through the rite, but vests for the eucharist in which the baptismal rite is situated.

As a side note, this is why one does not refer, in bulletins or other communications, to "Holy Baptism with Eucharist"—it is a nonsensical statement. Baptism takes place in the context of the eucharist, with the first communion of the newly baptized as the final and integral part of their initiation. (The only exception is for emergency baptism.) The liturgy is called "Holy Baptism," and the eucharistic context is assumed.

The props

Before the liturgy begins, the following are placed in readiness:

- The font or baptismal pool, which is partially filled with clean water
- One or more vessels of substantial size, filled with warm water
- The Altar Book, with the Thanksgiving over the Water marked
  (if it is to be sung)
- A glass vessel of chrism
- A towel to dry each candidate
- The paschal candle, standing near the font outside of Easter season or located near the lectern in Eastertide
- An alb or baptismal garment for each candidate (optional)
- A baptismal candle for each candidate (optional)
- A bowl of soapy water and a towel (or some suitable substitute) at the credence table, for the celebrant to remove chrism from the hands before the eucharistic prayer

The entrance rite

The lay assistants and clergy enter in procession. Upon arriving at the altar, the clergy reverence it with a deep bow. (If the celebrant is a bishop, she hands off the mitre and staff to an assistant first, for reasons of both practicality and piety.)

 Celebrating the Eucharist (Church Publishing, 2007) offers a detailed discussion of processions. The order for a baptism could include, in addition to the usual assistants and clergy, the baptismal candidates and sponsors:

Thurifer

Crucifer

Torch Torch

Choir

Candidate

Sponsors

Candidate

Sponsors

Deacon

Presider

 This has the admirable effect of highlighting the role of the baptismal candidates. Yet the candidates are not yet members of the body of Christ, and so one might conclude that it is inappropriate for them to process in with the liturgical ministers (though they might process *out* with them).

 Bishops, and more importantly, those working with them at an episcopal visit, will want to consult Paul Marshall's book *The Bishop Is Coming!* (Church Publishing, 2007) for relevant modifications to the ceremonial when a bishop presides in the baptismal liturgy, as only minimal notes will be given in this text.

The presider, standing in the usual place and facing the congregation, says the opening acclamation, and the people respond. The celebrant then, without announcing page numbers or otherwise interrupting the flow, leads the baptismal versicles and responses. The (optional) Gloria may be omitted. The presider prays the Collect of the Day, maintaining a distinct silence after the invitation and before the collect itself.

The entrance section of Holy Baptism is somewhat deceptive: it begins with a familiar opening acclamation, but then drops in the versicles and responses that are only used in baptism. It is reasonably effective to print the opening acclamation and the versicles in the bulletin, so that the flipping of pages might at least be minimized; this seems a compromise, but less destructive than announcing page numbers.

The BCP allows the *Gloria* to be sung after the opening versicles. While it is a festive gesture to sing it, it could well be omitted here. The *Gloria* was a later add-on to the liturgy, as the entrance rite mushroomed in the early Middle Ages. The opening versicles do a sufficient job of praising God and signaling the nature of the occasion.

Collects terminate prayer; they are not the sum total of prayer in and of themselves. That means that in the dialogue between celebrant and people ("The Lord be with you/And also with you/Let us pray"), one sees an actual invitation to the people to pray. It would be rude to invite the people to pray and then not allow them time to do just that. Therefore, the celebrant should maintain silence for a few seconds after "Let us pray" before saying the collect.

The Word liturgy

All are seated for the readings. The propers of the day are used. Two lessons, as indicated in the lectionary, are read, with a hymn, psalm, or anthem following each. The gospel is read by a deacon or assisting priest, with the usual ceremonies. The presider or some other person preaches the sermon. (If the presider is a bishop: the bishop is seated, wearing the mitre for the lessons. The bishop removes the mitre and, standing, holds the staff for the gospel reading.)

When baptism is reserved to the four appropriate calendrical occasions, plus the bishop's visit, as specified in the BCP, the propers of the day offer more than adequate material for a sermon that also addresses the nature of the ritual occasion. While the prayer book permits just one lesson before the gospel, it would be a strange omission to bypass one of the lectionary texts for such a significant occasion.

It is very important that readers have rehearsed adequately before the liturgy. This is especially true if sponsors, family members, or friends of the candidates have been asked to take part, and they are unaccustomed to reading in church. The proclamation of the word is a crucial part of the baptismal liturgy, and so the readers must be audible.

The gospel should be read with all of the ceremony to which the assembly is accustomed on festive occasions. In many places, this will mean a gospel procession with torches and incense (see *Celebrating the Eucharist* for a description of gospel processions). If the gospel is to be read in the midst of the congregation, or if it is to be processed to the ambo (or lectern/pulpit) to be read, it is important that the gospel book be seen as the significant symbolic object in the procession. This means that the cross should *not* be carried in the gospel procession.

No music, vocal or instrumental, intrudes between the reading of the gospel and the sermon. The sermon is meant to proceed from the gospel, and any interruption undermines that connection. Hymnody tends to substitute other texts as the last, lingering words in the hearer's mind before the sermon, in place of the gospel. Instrumental music, particularly a reprise of the melody of the sequence hymn before the gospel, amounts to little more than ecclesiastical elevator music, at once evoking the prior hymn-text and diminishing it. Either constitutes a distraction. There is no harm in a little pregnant silence between the reading and the preaching, and if congregations grow too uncomfortable with that small amount of silence, there is something at work on a deeper level that needs pastoral attention.

The sermon is on the texts of the day, and on the occasion. The preacher ought to be able to connect the two thematically.

The presentation and examination of the candidates

The celebrant moves to the center of the space and invites the candidates to be presented. (If the celebrant is a bishop, the bishop wears the mitre and is seated on a chair or faldstool in full view of the congregation.) Candidates and sponsors stand before the celebrant. The congregation may be asked to sit or to stand; the appropriate direction should be printed in the bulletin.

It is customary in most places for the congregation to be seated for the presentation of the candidates and to be asked to stand only before being asked to support the candidates. There is nothing wrong with this, but it also powerful for the entire congregation to stand in solidarity with the sponsors and candidates for the presentation.

Adult candidates (and older children) are presented individually, and after each presentation the celebrant asks the candidate if he desires to be baptized. Infants (and younger children) are then presented individually, with the celebrant asking each set of parents and godparents the questions about their role and responsibilities collectively. Next, the celebrant asks all older candidates and the sponsors of those unable to speak for themselves to make the renunciations of evil and the adhesions to Christ. Then, if there are candidates for confirmation, reception, or the reaffirmation of baptismal vows, the bishop invites them to be presented, and they come forward to stand alongside the baptismal candidates. They are asked collectively if they reaffirm their renunciation and their commitment to Christ. Finally, if the congregation has been seated for the preceding presentation, the celebrant asks all to stand. Then, the celebrant asks all present if they will support the candidates, to which the congregation responds in a loud voice. As each question is asked, the celebrant makes eye contact with the person or persons being queried.

The renunciations and adhesions in baptism are an important part of the rite. It is important to note that the Book of Common Prayer handles the presentations of the various sorts of candidates in quite distinct ways, differences that should be reflected in the performance of the rite. Adult candidates are presented individually and asked if they desire baptism in order to heighten the sense that this is a life-and-death matter. Once presented, the candidates should remain in a group in front of the celebrant, while other candidates come forward. Infant candidates do not have the chance to say a life-or-death "yes" themselves; they are presented individually by name instead. But the godparents' promises to raise the child in the Christian faith and life are not of the same order of significance as the adult candidates' affirmation of a desire to be baptized, and so it is reasonable that the godparents make their promises collectively. Finally, candidates for the various rites in reaffirmation of baptism are presented collectively, again because the reaffirmation of baptism is not of the same order of magnitude as baptism itself. There is no need to query these candidates individually.

A word about eye contact: the questions asked of the candidates in baptism are life-changing. The celebrant needs to treat them as real questions asked of real people, who might really say no, rather than a rote recitation. That means looking at the person to whom one is speaking. If the celebrant cannot memorize the questions, then an assistant might hold the book discreetly to the side, or the celebrant might look down at the book held in her hand to grab her line, then look up to deliver it. But under no circumstances should the celebrant look strictly at the book during the renunciations and adhesions.

The baptismal covenant

The celebrant leads the assembly in the recitation of the baptismal covenant, with the candidates and sponsors standing in a group at the front of the assembly. (If the celebrant is a bishop, she remains seated through the covenant.) The celebrant looks at the candidates during the queries.

The baptismal covenant is a crucial part of the church's theology and practice. The celebrant should treat each query as a real question to be asked and should look directly at the candidates, not at the prayer book, to suggest that the candidates' response actually matters.

Prayers for the candidates

The celebrant invites the assembly to prayer. The deacon or other person appointed leads the assembly in the prayers for the candidates. (If the celebrant is a bishop, at this point the bishop stands. The bishop removes the mitre if the prayers are said or sung while stationary. If the prayers are said or sung in procession, then the bishop wears the mitre.) If the font is at a distance from the place where the presentation occurred, the ministers, candidates, and sponsors process to the font during the prayers for the candidate, read by a deacon or sponsor. It is appropriate for the procession to be led by a server (or a second deacon) carrying the paschal candle, if it is in the Easter season. Outside of Eastertide, a server leads the candidates and sponsors, followed by the clergy.

The prayers for the candidate are in the form of a litany, which makes them appropriate to be said (or chanted) in procession. It is traditional for a deacon to lead the prayers of the people and other litanies. In the absence of a deacon, one of the sponsors could appropriately lead the prayers.

The paschal candle is carried to the font in the procession, if it is the Easter season. Outside of the Easter season, the candle will have been placed near the font before the liturgy begins. It is important that the paschal candle be seen as the dominant symbol in the procession, so it should never be accompanied by a cross and/or torches in the procession.

It is helpful if the litany covers the entire movement to the font, so the petitions should not be rushed. It is not a problem if the procession reaches the font well before the end of the litany.

Thanksgiving over the Water

The clergy, baptismal candidates, sponsors, and assistants stand around the font or pool in such a way that the obstruction of the congregation's view is minimized. (If the celebrant is a bishop, the bishop removes the mitre on arrival at the font, in preparation for the Thanksgiving over the Water.)

A server stands near the clergy to assist in handling books and vessels. A deacon, assisting priest, or the celebrant pours water from a large vessel into the font or pool. The font or pool is filled immediately before the Thanksgiving over the Water is said, not during it. Silence is kept while the water is poured, so that the sound of the rushing water may fill the room. Even if a large baptismal pool is used, it is helpful to pour a vessel of water into the font.

With a server holding the book (either the prayer book or, if the text is to be sung, the Altar Book), the celebrant chants or says the dialogue and the Thanksgiving over the Water. She extends hands in the orans position through the Thanksgiving, dropping hands out of the orans to extend hands, palms down, over the water and then lower them to touch it (tracing a sign of the cross if desired), at the words "Now sanctify this water. . . ." Alternatively, instead of tracing a cross the celebrant might dip cupped hands into the water and raise them to allow water to run through her fingers as the prayer is said.

The pouring of water needs to be done with attention to its sign-value. A good quantity of water, from a sizable vessel, should be used. One should *not* pour water *during* the prayer, as is too often seen—that obscures both the sound of the water and the words of the prayer. The water should be poured from a sufficient height to allow it to be seen and heard by the congregation.

The Thanksgiving over the Water is one of the most significant texts in the Book of Common Prayer. The dialogue at its beginning hints at its parallel to the eucharistic prayer, the other great thanksgiving prayer of the church. The use of the orans position visually reinforces this, and the extension of hands at "Now sanctify this water . . ." underscores the epiclesis in the prayer, as the Spirit is invoked over the water to sanctify it. The Thanksgiving should be chanted or said in a clear voice at an even pace, not rushed, so that the extravagant imagery can be appreciated.

Consecration of chrism

If a bishop is presiding, the chrism is consecrated. A glass vessel of significant size, containing olive oil mixed with chrism essence or oil of balsam in large quantity, is brought to the bishop by a server. The bishop lays a hand on the vessel and says the prayer, while a server holds the book. The bishop then puts on the mitre, after the blessing.

For the blessing of chrism to be meaningful, the oil must be present in quantity, so that as many as possible may see (and smell) it. If there is no bishop present, the chrism used at this liturgy will have been consecrated on a previous occasion.

The baptism

The baptismal washing may be done by the celebrant or an assisting priest or deacon. (If the celebrant is a bishop, the washing is normally done by assisting clergy, preferably one who has a pastoral relationship with the candidate.) If baptism is to be by immersion and the minister is to enter the baptismal pool along with the candidate, shoes and socks, as well as chasuble and stole, will need to be removed before entering. The chasuble and stole should be handed to a server, who will take them to the place where the minister is to change later. The minister enters the pool before the candidate is presented by name. If the minister is not to enter the pool, the minister simply stands alongside the

pool and rolls up the sleeves of her alb. A server stands near the minister, holding towels and candles (if desired). Sponsors present each candidate by name to the celebrant, or to an assisting priest or deacon who will do the actual administration of the water. If baptism is by immersion, the celebrant or assisting minister helps an adult candidate into the water. The candidate is immersed three times while the minister says the baptismal formula, "N., I baptize you. . . ." The minister should be able to say this from memory, but a server could hold the book if necessary. The candidate is helped up out of the water and given a towel by a server. If an infant candidate is to be immersed by a minister not standing in a pool, the minister rolls up the sleeves of the alb to the elbow. The infant is taken in the crook of the arm by the minister and then lowered into the font three times, taking care not to immerse the nose and mouth, while the minister says the baptismal formula. The candidate is given back to the parents or godparents, who are also given a towel by a server. If baptism is by pouring, an adult candidate bows *his head over the font while the minister pours water from the font, using a flagon or pitcher, over the head three times and says the baptismal formula. An infant candidate is held over the font by parents or sponsors (or, if desired, by the minister), while the minister pours water over the head three times and says the baptismal formula. In all cases, if baptism is done by pouring, it is done with a great deal of water. The server gives the candidate (or, in the case of an infant, her sponsor or parent) a towel.*

The practicalities of the worship space will dictate many of the choices made.

The flagon or pitcher used if one baptizes by pouring should be of moderate size. One that is too large will not be easily maneuvered with one hand when it is full. One that is too small will undercut the extravagant imagery of the Thanksgiving over the Water. The vessel to be used can be immersed three times in the font to fill it and then poured out three times, or it may be immersed once and then poured out in thirds as the baptismal formula is said.

One should not be too worried about water being splashed about, but there is some need to be concerned about safety in the event that a great deal of water is splashed on a stone or tile floor. One might place a large towel or two nearby for a server to deal with any slipping hazard either after the administration of water or at the peace. One should also be scrupulously careful about any electrical equipment in proximity to a baptismal pool or font, for obvious reasons.

Assuming that a significant amount of water is used, and particularly in the case of immersion, the newly baptized are taken behind a screen or to another room to change into dry clothes. Over their street clothes, adults and children may be robed in albs. Infants and toddlers may opt for white street clothes or, for those families for whom it is a custom, a baptismal dress.

If the minister accompanied the candidates into an immersion pool, the minister will need to change into dry clothes and a dry alb behind a screen or in another room. If this minister is not the presider of the rite (in other words, if she was an assisting priest or deacon), then the presider scoops water from the pool into a vessel, and with a sprig of evergreen or other implement sprinkles the assembly with baptismal water while processing back to the front of the church. If the minister who entered the pool is also the presider, the sprinkling may be delegated to an assisting priest or deacon, or the action may be delayed. In the latter case, the presider returns from having changed and goes directly to the pool, where she scoops up baptismal water in a vessel and sprinkles the assembly as she processes to the front of the church.

A hymn with a baptismal theme may be sung during this entire action, to cover the disappearance and reappearance of candidates (and clergy).

Private dressing areas are needed for each person. All those candidates (and parents, in the case of infant candidates) who exited to change return before the end of the hymn, processing directly to the front of the church if the font is in a place that is not in full view of the congregation.

This is a practical matter. Patrick Malloy suggests the singing of a baptismal hymn (and in particular, Hymn 296 in *Hymnal 1982*, "We know that Christ is raised and dies no more") to cover this action, noting that otherwise there is a purposeless silence.[19] It is possible that, if only infants are immersed, one might delay changing them until the peace, provided that they are wrapped in a large, dry towel for warmth directly after the immersion, but the discomfort of thoroughly wet clothes against the skin should not be underestimated.

Vesting the newly baptized in albs, while optional, is a custom that evokes the imagery of the saints robed in white, washed in the blood of the Lamb, in Revelation 7.

The baptismal sprinkling is an important, tactile reminder of the assembly's own baptisms, and it is evocative of the shared recitation of the baptismal covenant. It is therefore best not to omit it, even if the one to do the sprinkling must change clothes first.

If the font is not in full sight of the congregation, and if the minister and candidates did not exit to change, the baptismal party and clergy process back to the front of the church. Before departing, the presider takes some of the water from the font in a vessel and, using a sprig of evergreen or some other implement, sprinkles the congregation with baptismal water during the procession. If the font is in full view of the congregation, everyone stays in place for what follows.

Chrismation

The celebrant (without the mitre, if she is a bishop) prays over the newly baptized, extending hands while saying the prayer, "Heavenly Father, we thank you that by water and the Holy Spirit. . . ." *The presider (seated and wearing the mitre, if a bishop) then chrismates each candidate. A server brings the chrism to the presider. The presider pours chrism from the vessel directly onto the head of the newly baptized individual, returns the vessel, imposes both hands on the head, and traces the cross on the forehead with a thumb, saying, "N., you are sealed by the Holy Spirit in Baptism and marked as Christ's own for ever." The action is repeated for each individual. Alternatively, the presider pours chrism from the vessel into her own cupped hand, returns the vessel, then smears the chrism on the head and forehead of the newly baptized person. The presider then imposes both hands on the head of the individual and traces the cross on the (now oily) forehead with a thumb, while saying, "N., you are sealed. . . ." The action is repeated for each individual.*

The imposition of hands and chrismation after the water bath is part of the restoration of the ancient pattern of initiation in the 1979 BCP. Chrism should be used, even though the prayer book does permit its omission.

The Book of Common Prayer allows chrismation to take place immediately after the water bath and before the post-baptismal prayer for the gifts of the Spirit, "Heavenly Father. . . ." But this concession was first proposed to solve the supposed logistical difficulties in baptizing each candidate in turn and then going back to them to chrismate them. Massey Shepherd argued convincingly to the Standing Liturgical Commission that if the intent was to restore the ancient baptismal liturgy, then placing consignation and chrismation before the "Heavenly Father . . ." prayer would undercut the meaning of the action, which was intended to be the ancient laying-on-of-hands. The Standing Liturgical Commission heeded his argument; the option to relocate the chrismation only came with the Draft Proposed Book.[20] That editorial change represented a choice of supposed practicality over theological and liturgical integrity, and yet it was never clear that the logistics were that daunting to begin with. The option to relocate the consignation and chrismation allows one to flee from the implications of the 1979 BCP, with its restored rite of initiation, and so this is an option that is best not exercised. Efficiency is rarely the most important value to be considered in making choices about ritual.

When the chrism is used, it should be used in abundance, so that all may see (and smell) it. Baptism and its associated rites should overwhelm the senses—of touch, of hearing, of smell, and (at the communion) of taste. The more oil used in chrismation, the better.

The hand of the presider is placed on the head, in the ancient imposition of hands, and the thumb traces the cross in the now-oily forehead. If it is possible, it is best to make the gestures big—one should hand off the vessel of chrism to a server before the hand is imposed, so that *both* hands might be placed on the neophyte's head. This is a solemn moment, connecting our actions with those of Christians centuries past and evoking the abundant gift of the Holy Spirit, and so this action, no less than the water bath, needs to be done with the same serious joy and boldness as the immersion or pouring.

After an individual candidate is chrismated, a server may light a small candle from the paschal candle and give it to the candidate (or in the case of an infant, to her parent or sponsor). This is repeated for each individual candidate in turn, as each is chrismated.

Welcoming

After all the neophytes have been chrismated, the presider invites the congregation to welcome them. The congregation joins in saying the welcoming, "We receive you. . . ."

If the entire baptismal party did not return to the front of the church earlier, before the "Heavenly Father . . ." prayer, they do so now, after the welcoming and before the peace. The presider uses a vessel to scoop up some water from the font before departing, and, with a branch of evergreen or some other implement, sprinkles the congregation with baptismal water as the procession moves to the front of the church.

There should be no parading of infants by the presider or other clergy. The welcoming is the congregation's action, and so the presider functions only to cue the assembly's speaking part. It is best if the presider stays in the background for the welcoming. Ideally, there would be no parading of neophytes at all, but if it is to be done, it should be done by the sponsors, and adults should be paraded with every bit as much prominence as children. If the baptismal party is moving to the front of the church at this point, there is no separate parading (as it would be redundant). Rather, the procession back from the font serves the same purpose, and it does so in a way that treats all neophytes equitably.

At confirmation, reception, or reaffirmation

The newly baptized and their sponsors stand to the side or take their seats, as the candidates for confirmation/reception/reaffirmation come to stand in a group directly in front of the bishop. The bishop invites the assembly to prayer, then prays, "Almighty God, we thank you that by the death and resurrection. . . ." The bishop takes the mitre and is seated. Then each candidate comes individually and kneels before the bishop. The bishop is told the name of the candidate and the desired rite (confirmation, reception, or reaffirmation). The candidate lays hands on the head of each candidate and says the appropriate formula. After each candidate has been prayed over, the candidate rises and returns to stand with the group of other candidates at center. When all have received the imposition of hands, the bishop stands, removes the mitre, and prays, "Almighty and everliving God, let your fatherly hand. . . ."

The ceremonial elaboration of these rites is minimal, as confirmation has its origins in a modest blessing by the bishop, added onto elaborate baptismal ceremonies. The core of the rite is the imposition of hands by the bishop, with no additions or adjuncts. Chrism is not used, to avoid confusion with the post-baptismal hand-laying and chrismation restored to the baptismal rite. Sponsors do not join the bishop in imposing hands on candidates, to avoid obscuring the central ritual action, which is the imposition of the bishop's hands in blessing.

The bishop imposes hands on all candidates, because the text of each prayer reflects a blessing, and the imposition of hands was the ancient gesture used to reflect blessing.

Peace

The peace is exchanged. The presider takes care to greet the newly baptized first, then those who renewed their baptismal vows. Care is taken so that the peace does not become overlong, stretching out of proportion to its place in the liturgy.

The peace is a part of the initiatory rite. In the ancient church, in which catechumens were customarily dismissed from the assembly before the peace, this was a symbolic moment: the first sharing of the peace by the newly baptized. In our present day, this will generally not be the case, but it is nevertheless the first time that the newly baptized share the peace as a full member of the body. While it need not be overdone, the significance of the moment should not be forgotten.

At the eucharist

The liturgy continues with the offertory. Either at the peace or at the offertory but before handling anything to be placed on the altar, the celebrant uses a bowl of soapy water and towel, placed at the credence table, to wash chrism from the hands. The newly baptized (if adults) bring forward the bread and wine. If there are many more adult candidates than loaves and vessels of wine, some may bring forward the money and other gifts. They hand these directly to the deacon or assisting priest setting the table (or to the celebrant, if there are no assisting clergy and the celebrant sets the table).

During the eucharistic prayer, if Prayer D is used, the newly baptized and newly confirmed are included in the diptychs (the optional sentences that begin with "remember," at the end of the prayer). The diptychs may be read by a deacon, or a concelebrating or assisting priest.

At the distribution of communion, great care is taken so that the newly baptized receive the bread and wine immediately after the presider and other ministers of communion.

The prayer book allows the liturgy to continue with the prayers of the people (and then presumably to include the confession) before the offertory. But this is structurally anomalous. The prayers for the candidates function, as in other "ritual masses," as the prayers of the people. To resume at the prayers of the people would disrupt the flow of the ritual action, and so it is best to flow from peace to offertory, as in the ordinary structure of the eucharist on all other occasions.

It is helpful to have the newly baptized present the bread and wine, and other offerings. This highlights their role and participation in the assembly, as they now perform representative actions of the whole assembly and join in symbolically offering their life and labors to the Lord. While it would be tempting to some to have them, and any other candidates, stand at the altar for the eucharistic prayer, this would unnecessarily crowd the altar and send a confusing message. It is best for them to rejoin the assembly after delivering the bread and wine (and other gifts), so that all join in the great thanksgiving according to their roles. The presider, after all, is simply servant and spokesperson for the assembly, so that there is no greater dignity in standing closer to the altar.

It is very important that the newly baptized receive communion first, because it is the reception of communion that completes the initiatory process. Receiving first highlights this. Further, all neophytes need to receive communion, not just adults and older children. Not to communicate infants and younger children at their own baptisms is to delay their participation in the life of the body into which they have just been initiated, and it puts the lie to all of our theological statements about baptism being full initiation. The ancient form of initiation involved three elements: the water bath, the hand-laying and anointing, and first communion. To omit any of these is to impoverish the rite, so it is very important that infants be given their first communion at their baptisms.

The practicalities of communicating infants will be discussed in chapter six.

The dismissal is said from the altar, before the procession out—not from the back of the church.

While those seeking a practical guide to eucharistic ceremonial should consult Patrick Malloy's *Celebrating the Eucharist*, the rubrics of the prayer book do not anticipate anything being inserted between the blessing and dismissal. Dismissing the congregation from the altar has an important symbolic resonance: the people are sent forth into the world from the altar at which they have been fed. This is far more evocative than the dismissal uttered at the back door, directed at the back of the people's heads. If Christian initiation is, as the prayer book asserts, about living as a disciple of Christ in the world, then the dismissal is too important to bury at the back door.

At the conclusion of the liturgy, the newly baptized (with infants being carried by parents) may join in the exiting procession, directly in front of the deacon and presider. If the clergy customarily stand at the door to greet folks after worship, the newly baptized might stand and greet folks.

Baptism is the incorporation of a person into a dynamic relationship with the living God, through the paschal mystery of Christ's life, death, and resurrection. While God's grace is at work in the lives of catechumens long before they come to the font, and while the work of formation and growth in the life of faith—growing into the full stature of Christ, to paraphrase the Apostle Paul—is ongoing, baptism is a watershed moment. It needs to be celebrated as such. Indeed, while in many Episcopal parishes our worship life has come to be centered in the eucharist, that sacrament is really the renewal (in terms of both "reaffirmation" and "rejuvenation") of our baptismal vows. We need, therefore, to take great care in the administration of baptism. Its symbols should sing—they should be so big that they overwhelm the senses. Its performance should rightly be seen as a high point of a parish's life.

In the next chapter, we will take up the problem of what to do with the renewal of baptismal vows in the rites of confirmation, reception, and reaffirmation. These cognate rites should never overshadow baptism, from which they draw their meaning and rationale.

Notes

1. Robert Hovda, *Strong, Loving, and Wise: Presiding in Liturgy* (Collegeville, MN: Liturgical Press, 1976), 39.

2. See Marshall, "Trite Rite," 71.

3. BCP 1979, 298, 312.

4. Talley, *Origins of the Liturgical Year*, 34–36; Paul F. Bradshaw, "'Diem baptismo sollemniorem': Initiation and Easter in Christian Antiquity" in *Living Water, Sealing Spirit: Readings on Christian Initiation*, ed. Maxwell Johnson (Collegeville, MN: Liturgical Press, 1995), 137–44, 180–85; Bradshaw, "Baptismal Practice in the Alexandrian Tradition: Eastern or Western?" in Johnson, ed., *Living Water, Sealing Spirit*, 83–87.

5. Johnson, *Rites of Christian Initiation*, 180–85.

6. BOS, 114, 116, 122.

7. BCP 1979, 265; Talley, *Origins of the Liturgical Year*, 174.

8. Bradshaw, "Diem baptismo sollemniorem," 138–39, 143–45; Talley, *Origins of the Liturgical Year*, 127–28; Johnson, *Rites of Christian Initiation*, 53–54, 168.

9. Talley, *Origins of the Liturgical Year*, 127–28; Johnson, *Rites of Christian Initiation*, 53–54, 168; Bradshaw, "Diem baptismo sollemniorem," 143–44.

10. Meyers, *Continuing the Reformation*, 195.

11. BCP 1979, 412.

12. See, for example, Hovda, *Strong, Loving, and Wise*, 73–74.

13. Hovda, *Strong, Loving, and Wise*, 74.

14. Hatchett, *Commentary*, 276.

15. BOS, 209.

16. Marshall, *Trite Rite*, 74.

17. This is attributed variously, but can be credited to John A. T. Robinson, "Preface," in *Making the Building Serve the Liturgy: Studies in the Re-Ordering of Churches*, ed. Gilbert Cope (London: Mowbray, 1962); see James F. White, "A Protestant Worship Manifesto," *Christian Century* 99 (January 27, 1982): 86.

18. Aidan Kavanagh, *Elements of Rite: A Handbook of Liturgical Style* (New York: Pueblo Books, 1982), 18.

19. Patrick Malloy, *Celebrating the Eucharist: A Practical Ceremonial Guide for Clergy and Other Liturgical Ministers* (New York: Church Publishing, 2007), 215.

20. Meyers, *Continuing the Reformation*, 181, 184.

Chapter 5

_____

PERFORMING THE SOLEMN RENEWAL OF BAPTISMAL PROMISES

Confirmation survived the last revision of the Book of Common Prayer, despite the efforts of liturgical scholars and theologians. In theory, the church could still choose to eliminate it, but it shows little interest in doing so, having in the 2012 General Convention tabled legislation that would have removed confirmation as a qualification for office-holding. Regardless of such legislative decisions, there are choices one can make to improve the way that confirmation is implemented and understood.

RECASTING CONFIRMATION, RECEPTION, AND REAFFIRMATION

As we have seen, the ancient initiatory process had involved, at least in the West by the fourth century, a water bath, followed by the imposition of hands. In the course of the Middle Ages, these two components broke apart, with the hand-laying becoming the separate rite of confirmation. Once the 1979 BCP restored hand-laying to the baptismal rite, confirmation lost its most ancient rationale: that it was the sacramental completion of baptism, the imposition of hands that had become detached from baptism. For those who have seen confirmation as an "owning of the covenant," as one assumes baptismal promises for one's self, the eucharist (properly understood) offers a similar and more frequent opportunity

[handwritten margin notes: "4x baptisms / Bapt of Lord / Easter Vigil / Pentecost / all Saints / Visitation"]

[handwritten margin note: "Where?"]

to recall one's baptism, while the quarterly renewal of baptismal vows prescribed by the 1979 prayer book does so even more effectively. Confirmation's former functions are thus fulfilled by other rites.

Yet for all that many liturgical scholars would love to get rid of confirmation as a separate rite, it is unlikely that confirmation, reception, and reaffirmation will disappear completely anytime soon. This is not entirely a bad thing. Indeed, confirmation, reception, and reaffirmation can serve a useful pastoral function.

There may be a point or points in time when it is pastorally appropriate for an individual to ritualize a deepening or renewed commitment to living the life of a baptized person. Fundamentally, this is what confirmation, reception, and the reaffirmation of baptismal vows are all about. This is true even of the rite of reception, which, when the liturgical text is read closely, is clearly seen to be a recognition of the candidate's baptism and a renewal of that person's baptismal promises, rather than a passage into a new status. What confirmation, reception, and reaffirmation do offer, in fact, is a means to ritualize one's commitment to one's baptismal vows.

Because these rites are about giving ritual expression to a deeper or renewed commitment, the church must be careful to avoid encouraging the idea that they are part of a inexorable progression that everyone necessarily will undergo. Indeed, it would have been best if the prayer book had never articulated an expectation that everyone would be confirmed.[1] This was an insertion made by the House of Bishops at the 1973 General Convention; originally, the rubrics would simply have indicated that *some* might choose to make such an affirmation.[2] The language of "expectation" tends to locate confirmation as a part of the life cycle, leading to the present-day confirmation machine, observable in some parishes, which cranks teenagers through an educational curriculum before spitting them out under the bishop's hands. Such expectations do little to help the candidates or the congregation see confirmation as an act of free will, undertaken by autonomous adults, in affirmation of baptism.

[handwritten margin note: "BCP 412"]

Careful preparation and performance of the rite can add clarity. Confirmation is a public reaffirmation of one's baptismal promises—nothing less, but nothing more. The essential liturgical action is the imposition of hands by the bishop after a public recommitment to baptismal promises.

Visitation Customary

What follows are brief suggestions for the performance of confirmation. Those seeking a more thorough treatment should consult Paul Marshall's book *The Bishop Is Coming!*, a guide to the entirety of a bishop's parish visitation, including baptism and confirmation.

RITUAL PREPARATION

All of the admonitions on the performance of baptism apply here. In addition, great care must be taken to ensure that the rite does not overshadow baptism, particularly if both baptisms and confirmations take place in the same liturgy. In the ritual formation of candidates for the rites of reaffirmation, it will be important that they have a sense of the occasion and its meaning—and since one is supposed to be "mature" to be confirmed, to reaffirm, or to be received, this is a higher bar than that set for baptism. Paradoxically, candidates will need to understand both the importance of their renewal of baptismal vows and its subordination to baptism itself. The rite is derivative of baptism, not a completion of it, and certainly not something surpassing it, never mind the woman or man in a mitre who presides at the rite.

SCHEDULING

Scheduling poses some difficulties, due to the bishops' monopoly, at present, on confirmation. Most parishes will not have a choice about when the bishop shows up; confirmations will happen at that time, regardless of season or of convenience. That said, adults who were baptized at the Vigil *if there was not a bishop present* should, so far as possible, be confirmed by the bishop within the fifty days of Easter season. (A bishop celebrating baptism at the Vigil would have imposed hands and chrismated the neophyte after the water bath. In this case, the person is not subsequently confirmed, because she or he has already received the laying on of hands by a bishop after a mature profession of faith.) It would be ideal if all candidates who have taken part in a catechumenal process of preparation could be confirmed, received, or make their reaffirmation within the Great Fifty Days, even if this requires regional confirmations. The link between Easter and baptism is too important, as is the connection between the catechumenate cycle and the church year. One should at least avoid Lent, as the time in which one properly prepares for initiatory rites but does not undergo them.

The other concerns in scheduling baptism do not apply here. Mercifully, many parishes have multiple candidates for these rites in a given year, so that the cult of "specialness" has not distorted confirmation as it has distorted baptism in some places.

Sign-value

The essential sign in confirmation is the imposition of hands by the bishop. This should be the principal element in the rite of confirmation; nothing should obscure that action. Having been used lavishly in baptism, chrism is at best redundant and at worst misleading in confirmation. Because hand-laying was an ancient gesture of blessing, it is perfectly appropriate—and indeed, desirable—that the same hand-laying gesture be used in reception and reaffirmation, as all three formulae resemble a blessing.

The hand-laying gesture, precisely because it is the core liturgical action in a rite that is otherwise devoid of symbols, must be done with clarity and vigor. This argues in favor of imposing two hands, not just one.

Avoiding too much fuss

At the end of the day, confirmation, reception, and reaffirmation are pastoral rites. They can provide an important opportunity for an individual to ritualize a turn in their spiritual journey, whether it be a first, mature commitment to vows made by others on one's behalf when an infant, or a renewed commitment to one's own promises made some time ago. Such pastoral occasions can be significant in the life of an individual, and the liturgies and the persons who take part demand the care and attention of the clergy. But one must not confuse these pastoral rites with the rite of initiation (baptism) that brought them into the body of Christ. In the event that there are candidates for baptism as well as those for confirmation/reception/reaffirmation present, one must take care to ensure that the baptismal candidates are the center of attention. It is the making of vows for the first time that should have pride of place. Similarly, the festivities accompanying confirmation/reception/reaffirmation, such as at a parish reception or coffee hour, should not overshadow the festivities on baptismal occasions.

CEREMONIAL COMMENTARY ON THE RITE OF CONFIRMATION/RECEPTION/REAFFIRMATION, WHEN THERE IS NO BAPTISM

The ceremonies accompanying the rite of confirmation/reception/reaffirmation are rather more austere than those surrounding baptism. What follows is one approach to ritualizing the occasion; provided that one remembers that "less is more," other possibilities might well be used.

Furniture

Unlike baptism, little special equipment is required. The bishop will need a chair from which to preside from the presentation of the candidates until the peace. The rest of the time, the bishop should use the chair normally used by the celebrant in the parish eucharist (and not one of the special "bishop's chairs"[3] that sprouted like kudzu in ordinary parishes over the last century or so). Too often, the normal place of presiding poses challenges in terms of sight-lines; in these situations another chair may need to be placed at the center, facing the congregation, for this portion of the liturgy. The best solution is generally a "faldstool," a portable, folding stool that is unobtrusive when not occupied and that can be whisked away at the peace, when it is no longer needed.

Vesture

Clergy and lay assistants vest, from the beginning of the liturgy, as they would for the eucharist: alb, with stole for the clergy and chasuble for the presider. A deacon may wear a dalmatic. Just like baptism, the confirmation liturgy is a liturgical unity, and so one does not change vesture part way through the rite but vests for the eucharist in which confirmation is situated. Confirmation is structured as a "ritual mass"—essentially, a eucharist with special business embedded in it. Therefore, church bulletins should never use the phrase, "Confirmation and Eucharist."

The proper eucharistic vesture of a bishop is alb, stole, and chasuble, with mitre. The insignia of the ring and staff are also used. The popular image of a bishop in cope and mitre is a historical peculiarity in some ways. The cope is a vestment worn for liturgical processions of the free-standing kind, such as a rogation procession, and it might be worn for solemn evensong. It is not eucharistic garb, and therefore it should not be used in the initiation rites *unless* eucharist is to be omitted (for some unfathomable reason). Aidan Kavanagh – like

It is theoretically possible, though not at all desirable, for the bishop to preside over the confirmations but not at the eucharist itself. In this case, the bishop might vest in alb, stole, cope, and mitre, presiding through the first part of the liturgy and then being seated at the peace. After the peace, the only duty remaining for the bishop would be to pronounce the blessing. This arrangement is so anomalous that it would only be contemplated in the case of great infirmity on the part of the bishop, who finds himself able to sit but not to stand at the altar. Better to reschedule the confirmations for another day.

The practice of wearing rochet and chimere at eucharistic rites is roughly analogous to the practice of wearing cassock and surplice. It is a historical accident, resulting from the Reformation's rejection of eucharistic vesture. Rochet and chimere are choir dress, and so they should be used for noneucharistic liturgies, such as the daily office, and for liturgies at which the bishop is present but not presiding. Wearing a stole with rochet and chimere is not advisable, as the stole really belongs to a different type of vesture.

The props

Props are few and far between. In confirmation, there is no rubric directing the candidates be presented by name to the celebrant, and so one might contemplate using nametags or index cards printed with the name, to be held up in front of the bishop as the formula is being said. Such a practice would require the labels to be prepared before the liturgy. But unless there is an agreed-upon phonetic system, written labels invite Murphy to the liturgy. Better practice would be for a sponsor or assisting clergy person (preferably the one who has overseen the preparation of the candidates) to announce the names audibly, together with the desired rite (whether confirmation, reception, or reaffirmation).

The prayer book does not anticipate that chrism would be used in any manner in confirmation, but some bishops nevertheless do so. If it is to be used, then one will need chrism in a glass vessel of significance. One will also need a means for the bishop to clean her hands. It would be advisable to have a small hand towel placed near the bishop's faldstool, to blot up excess chrism after the confirmations and before the peace, as well as a bowl of soapy water and a towel at the credence table, for the bishop to use to before the eucharistic prayer. But again, the use of chrism in confirmation is to be discouraged.

The entrance rite

The lay assistants and clergy enter in procession. Upon arriving at the altar, the assisting clergy reverence it with a deep bow. The bishop hands off the mitre and staff to an assistant first, for reasons of both practicality and piety, and then bows deeply.

The presence of the bishop complicates the procession only slightly:

Thurifer

Crucifer

Torch Torch

Choir

Lay assistants

[Deacons who are not assisting]

[Presbyters who are not to stand at the altar]

Deacons who are assisting

Presbyters who will stand at the altar

Bishop's chaplain

Bishop

[two attending Deacons, if desired]

The bishop, standing in the usual place and facing the congregation, says the opening acclamation, and the people respond. The bishop then, without announcing page numbers or otherwise interrupting the flow, leads the baptismal versicles and responses. The (optional) Gloria may be omitted. The bishop prays the Collect of the Day.

The entrance section of confirmation is, like Holy Baptism, prone to lead congregations astray with its opening, as the familiar opening acclamation is followed by the baptismal versicles and responses. The temptation to announce page numbers, as a way of warning that the rite is a bit different than the usual form, should be resisted. It is preferable to print the opening acclamation and the versicles in the bulletin.

The prayer book allows the *Gloria* to be sung after the opening versicles, but this is a festive add-on that might be omitted. (It would be delightful to retain it for historical reasons, though, as once upon a time the *Gloria* was only sung when the bishop was present.)

It should be remembered that collects *terminate* prayer. The celebrant invites the congregation to pray with "Let us pray"; it is rude not to allow time for that prayer to happen. Therefore, a bit of silence is maintained between "Let us pray" and the collect that follows. If this is not the usual custom in a parish, the bishop should not be deterred. The bishop knows what she is doing, and it provides a teaching moment for the parish clergy.

The Word liturgy

The propers of the day are used. Two lessons, as indicated in the lectionary, are read, with a hymn, psalm, or anthem following each. The gospel is read by a deacon or assisting priest, with the usual ceremonies. The presider or some other person preaches the sermon.

The gospel should be read with all of the ceremony to which the assembly is accustomed. In many places, this will mean a gospel procession with torches and incense. If the gospel is to be read in the midst of the congregation, or if it is to be processed to the ambo (or lectern/pulpit) to be read, it is important to remember that the gospel book is itself the chief symbol in the procession. The cross, therefore, should *not* be carried in the gospel procession.

If incense is used, the thurible is brought to the bishop to be charged. The bishop is seated for this.

The deacon may seek the bishop's blessing before departing in the procession. While the deacon is empowered to read the gospel by virtue of ordination and therefore needs no further charge or permission, this is a harmless custom. The bishop is seated to deliver the blessing, and the deacon comes before her and bows or kneels. The bishop lays hands on the deacon's head or makes the sign of the cross, saying "The Lord be in your heart and on your lips, that you may worthily proclaim his Gospel, in the name of the Father, and of the Son, and of the Holy Spirit." Once the procession has departed, the bishop stands and hands the mitre to an assistant. The bishop receives the staff and holds it with both hands for the reading of the gospel.

No music, of any sort, intrudes between the reading of the gospel and the sermon. The sermon is meant to proceed from the gospel, without interruption. Neither hymnody nor instrumental music is helpful in maintaining the assembly's focus on the gospel just read.

The sermon is on the texts of the day, and on the occasion, with the preacher connecting the two. Bishops will face greater challenges than presbyters in this, for the simple reason that baptisms are reserved to four calendrical occasions with baptismal themes, or when the bishop is present. A presbyter, therefore, has lectionary texts that are perfect for the occasion, while a bishop, whether preaching at baptism or confirmation, faces the choice between the random forces of the lectionary or the generic propers for those rites.

While the propers for confirmation may be used, it would be best for the bishop to preach on the normal lectionary cycle, so that the readings and sermon fit within the congregation's larger pattern of scripture reading. Further, the very thought of a bishop being forced to preach on the same confirmation propers week after week until Jesus returns or confirmation is abolished (whichever comes first) might well deter otherwise qualified candidates from the episcopate.

[handwritten marginal note: writes like Aidan Kavanagh in Elements of Rite - LOL]

The presentation and examination of the candidates

The bishop moves to the center of the space, takes the mitre, is seated in a chair or faldstool, and invites the candidates to be presented. Candidates and presenters stand before the celebrant. The congregation may stand here or be seated; direction will need to be given in the service bulletin. Candidates are presented collectively. They are asked collectively if they reaffirm their renunciation of evil and their commitment to Christ. If the congregation was seated for the examination, they now stand. Finally, the bishop asks all present if they will support the candidates, to which the congregation responds in a loud voice. At each point, the bishop looks directly at those being asked a question.

The renewal of the renunciations and adhesions in baptism are an important part of the rite, alongside the recitation of the baptismal covenant constituting its essential purpose.

It is significant that the prayer book requires that baptismal candidates be presented individually, by name, while requiring candidates for confirmation, reception, and reaffirmation to be presented as a group. The reaffirmation of baptism is not of the same order of magnitude as baptism itself.

Nevertheless, the questions of the candidate that follow are real and should not be minimized. The bishop makes eye contact with those being queried, because these are meaningful questions, not a rote recitation of a ritual text, and these questions are at the heart of the reaffirmation of baptismal vows.

The Baptismal Covenant

The bishop leads the assembly in the recitation of the baptismal covenant, with the candidates and sponsors standing in a group at the front of the assembly.

The baptismal covenant is a crucial part of the church's theology and practice, and its recitation here lies at the heart of confirmation's purpose: the solemn renewal of baptismal vows. The questions should not be rushed, and the bishop should make eye contact with the candidates. It may be helpful for an assistant to hold the book close to eye level, if the bishop cannot ask the questions without the text before him.

Prayers for the candidates

The bishop stands, removes the mitre, and invites the assembly to prayer. The deacon or other person appointed leads the assembly in the prayers for the candidates, and it is suggested that these be the prayers for the candidates from the liturgy for baptism. The bishop prays the concluding collect.

The prayers for the candidates are in the form of a litany. It is traditional for a deacon to lead these prayers. In the absence of a deacon, a layperson who had sponsored or otherwise prepared candidates would be a fitting person to lead them. The concluding collect, with its themes of covenant renewal and empowerment for service, offers a fairly succinct statement of the traditional purpose of confirmation.

Imposition of hands

The bishop takes the mitre and is seated. Then each candidate comes individually and kneels before the bishop. The bishop is told the name of the candidate and the desired rite (confirmation, reception, or reaffirmation). The bishop lays two hands on the head of each candidate and says the appropriate formula. After each candidate has been prayed over, the candidate rises and returns to stand with the group of other candidates at center. When all have received the imposition of hands, the bishop stands, removes the mitre, and prays, "Almighty and everliving God, let your fatherly hand. . . ."

The ceremonial elaboration of these rites is minimal, as confirmation has its origins in a modest blessing by the bishop, added onto elaborate baptismal ceremonies.[4] The core of the rite is the imposition of hands by the bishop, with no additions or adjuncts.

It is highly desirable that chrism not be used, to avoid confusion with the post-baptismal hand-laying and chrismation restored to the baptismal rite. Nevertheless, if chrism is used for confirmation candidates, then it should be used for all candidates who renew their baptismal promises, i.e., the candidates for reception and reaffirmation as well. All of them are making a solemn renewal of baptismal promises, and so the logic that allows a repetition of baptismal chrismation for confirmation candidates would necessarily require the chrismation of the other candidates as well.

Presenters/sponsors do not join the bishop in imposing hands on candidates, to avoid obscuring the central ritual action, which is the imposition of the *bishop's* hands in blessing. The bishop functions here as a representative of the wider church, recognizing the baptism of the candidates and receiving their solemn renewal of their vows. The sponsors do not have that same symbolic role. Indeed, when this sort of joining-in has taken place, it can resemble either a rugby scrum or the gang of presbyters clustering around the candidate at the ordination of a new priest. The latter is the more pernicious image, in that it can inadvertently reinforce the faulty theology that paints confirmation as "lay ordination." Similarly, the practice in some congregations (perhaps borrowed from certain Roman Catholic parishes) of investing the newly confirmed with a "confirmation stole" is a clericalizing turn to be resisted at all costs.

The bishop imposes hands on all candidates, whether for confirmation, reception, or reaffirmation, because the text of each prayer reflects a blessing, and the imposition of hands was the ancient gesture used to indicate blessing. It is also important to impose hands on those being received because of the wording of one canon: Canon I.17.1(d) states, "Those who have previously made a mature public commitment in another Church may be received by the laying on of hands by a Bishop of this Church, rather than confirmed." The practice observed in some places, in which the bishop shakes hands with those being received, would appear to be ruled out by the canon. Shaking hands with those being received is in any case a far weaker gesture than the prayerful imposition of hands.

The concluding prayer is said over those who were just confirmed. Confirmands should not return to their seats until after the peace, so that they may conveniently exchange the peace with the bishop.

Peace

The peace is exchanged. The bishop greets those who renewed their baptismal vows. Care is taken so that the peace does not become overlong, stretching out of proportion to its place in the liturgy.

The peace is, symbolically speaking, less significant in confirmation than it is in baptism, as the confirmands have been full members of the body of

Christ since their baptisms and therefore will have exchanged the peace with other members of the body for some time. Nevertheless, it is fitting that the confirmands exchange the peace with the bishop who has just prayed over them. They should do so before finding family and friends in the congregation to greet.

The peace is, at root, a ritualized greeting, not the seventh-inning stretch, and it needs to be kept within limits. It will be difficult, though not impossible, for a bishop to assert these limits in a congregation that has ignored them for years.

Announcements following the peace, unless limited to those that are absolutely necessary (a brief welcome to visitors, instructions about receiving communion), can have the effect of further derailing the liturgical flow.

At the eucharist

The liturgy continues with the offertory. The newly confirmed bring forward the bread and wine, money, and other gifts. They hand these directly to the deacon or assisting priest setting the table.

During the eucharistic prayer, if Prayer D is used, the newly confirmed are included in the "diptychs" (the memorials at page 375 in the prayer book). The diptychs may be read by a deacon, or by a concelebrating or assisting priest as the bishop may desire.

The prayer book allows the liturgy to continue with the prayers of the people (and then presumably to include the confession), before the offertory. But this is a structural anomaly best avoided. The prayers for the candidates function, as in other "ritual masses," as the prayers of the people. It is best to flow from peace to offertory, as in the normal structure of the eucharist on all other occasions.

It is helpful to have the newly confirmed present the bread and wine, and other offerings. This highlights their role and participation in the assembly, as they now perform representative actions of the whole assembly and join in symbolically offering their life and labors to the Lord. They rejoin the assembly after delivering the bread and wine (and other gifts), so that all take part in the Great Thanksgiving according to their roles.

FINAL THOUGHTS

Overall, the most helpful admonition to keep in mind is that of Aidan Kavanagh when he said that confirmation is a thing about which too much ought not be made. It can be a highly significant, deeply moving pastoral event in one's life. It can ritualize a significant turn in one's Christian journey. But it is not, cannot, and ought not be a substitute or rival for baptism, in its theological, ecclesiological, or liturgical roles in the life of the church and of the individual. This means that the celebration of confirmation needs to be kept in balance, so that it does not risk overshadowing baptism. Even though the bishop is present, the ceremonies of the occasion ought not send the implicit message that this rite matters more than the waters of new life.

Notes

1. BCP 1979, 412.

2. Meyers, *Continuing the Reformation*, 175.

3. There is properly only one "bishop's chair" in each diocese, and it is the *cathedra*, located at the cathedral church.

4. See Kavanagh, *Confirmation*.

Chapter 6

RETHINKING WHAT FOLLOWS: BAPTISM AND THE TABLE

Baptism is, in a sense, just the beginning. It inaugurates a relationship, bringing a person into new life in Christ. What follows is the lifelong struggle to live the Christian faith and life, as reflected in the baptismal covenant. The candidate for baptism promises to continue in the faith of the apostles and to serve others; she also promises to share in the eucharist ("the breaking of bread and the prayers").[1] In Anglican sacramental theology, the two sacraments (baptism and eucharist) are tightly linked. We therefore need to wrestle with two questions implied by baptism: is baptism the prerequisite for communion, and if so, is it the *only* prerequisite? As of this writing, the headline-grabbing question is whether the unbaptized may be admitted to the table, but at the same time, in some parishes not all the baptized participate fully in the eucharist. In this chapter, we will explore the relationship between baptism and eucharist, with an eye toward the basic question of who is to be admitted to the table.

COMMUNION OF THE UNBAPTIZED

As we have seen in chapter one, baptism was not always the gate to communion in Anglicanism. Either catechizing or confirmation served in that role until the mid-twentieth century, culminating in 1970 when the church officially removed confirmation as a requirement for communion. Over the ensuing decades, some fought a rear-guard action, insisting that one must both be baptized and "understand" the eucharist, but it was accepted by more and more that baptism was the sole prerequisite to communion. When one spoke of "open communion" in the 1970s and 80s, one meant to describe the practice of giving communion to baptized persons of other denominations. But by the end of the twentieth century and the beginning of the twenty-first, the discussion had shifted. Today, the cutting-edge question about access to communion concerns whether one should require baptism first, and "open communion" is taken to describe the practice of communicating the unbaptized. (It may be preferable to speak of "communion-before-baptism.") While the canons of the Episcopal Church prohibit giving communion to the unbaptized, and the 2012 General Convention reaffirmed the normative requirement of baptism before communion, the debate is likely to persist. A brief review of the arguments is in order.

Those in favor of giving communion to the unbaptized tend to make their case around two issues. First, there is the issue of hospitality: proponents argue that it is a breach of hospitality to exclude the unbaptized from communion. Such exclusion, one noted theologian has argued, is even worse now that the normative liturgical worship in Episcopal churches on Sundays and major feasts is eucharistic: "The gathered community is now very clearly defined by the community gathered for the eucharist in a way that was not the case before; to be excluded from it is therefore to be excluded from the church. The U.S. context . . . is bound to foment this sense of simple exclusion on the part of unbaptized adults not permitted to the communion rail."[2] Similarly, Sara Miles, in her memoir *Take This Bread*, frames the expectation of baptism before communion as an out-and-out barrier: "In most churches . . . the baptismal font is planted at the entrance . . . making it clear to visitors that initiation is required before receiving bread and wine. The font serves as a gate to keep the wrong people from the feast, and the Table remains mysterious and distant, something only priests can approach."[3] The metaphor of the gate is one that could be read in a different way, but proponents of communion-before-baptism see the font as a tool of exclusion.

Theologians have tried to stretch beyond hospitality alone, to try to find a greater significance than mere "niceness" to justify communion of the unbaptized.

Often, they appeal to the idea that communion-before-baptism shows God's unconditional grace; conversely, to exclude the unbaptized is seen by them as denying the graceful initiative of God. Baptism then becomes a response to the grace experienced in communion.[4] Another line of argument has been to expand the definition of "children of God" beyond the baptized. One writer, for example, rejects any distinctions between the baptized and unbaptized, arguing, "some cannot be 'more children of God' than others."[5] This would have puzzled many in the early church, not least the apostle Paul, who wrote in Galatians 3:26–27 of Christians having been adopted in baptism: "in Christ Jesus you are all children of God through faith. As many of you as were baptized into Christ have clothed yourselves with Christ."[6] Paul saw the primary identity marker of a Christian as being grounded in baptism—that is why he wrote so movingly of all other human distinctions (slave/free, Greek/Jew, man/woman) being overcome.

Boundaries play a crucial role in creating and maintaining identity. Boundaries are really identity markers: they signify the limit between those who share in an identity and those who do not. The point of Paul's words to the Galatians was not that all boundaries had ceased to be, but that the primary identity marker of baptism had erased all *other* boundaries. James Farwell notes:

> Clear boundaries do make possible good relations; conversely, it is difficult to enter into a healthy and genuine relationship with other persons or participate in the corporate practice of a group without clarity about their nature and purpose. Anthropology, ritual studies, and psychology confirm this folk wisdom that boundaries are essential to a coherent, even if flexible, sense of identity. . . . Challenging the differentiation represented by boundaries as an assault on the gospel is a category error: the function of boundaries is not necessarily judgment or exclusion, but definition and even invitation.[7]

Any sense of identity itself sets a boundary, distinguishing those who share in that identity from those who do not. By definition, some are "in" and some are "out," or rather, some share in the identity and some do not. One cannot create or maintain an identity without a sense of boundaries, however they may be defined.

Some have tried to use the church's practice of infant baptism to press home the case for communion of the unbaptized. The argument is roughly this: infant baptism reflects the idea that God's love comes through the community, apart from any response that the infant candidate can make. God, working through the community, eventually leads the infant candidate to the point of being able to make a response. In the same way, then, communion without baptism brings the recipient into the community, without the response of faith. Eventually, the person comes to the point of being able to make such a response.[8]

Unfortunately, this argument from infant baptism draws a false parallel, based on the faulty assumption that infant baptism is a *liturgical norm*, that which gives shape and meaning to the church's rites. By contrast, the liturgical norm in the Episcopal Church, as in the Roman Catholic Church, is adult baptism: infant baptism is seen as a permissible *departure* from the norm.[9] Such departures do not reflect fully the underlying theology of the rite, and so by definition one would not want to use them as the basis for an argument. To make sense of infant baptism, theologians from the time of the early church have pointed out that the assent of faith expected from an adult candidate is still made, though by the sponsors. Faithful assent remains part of baptism. Thus, infant baptism is not, as some assert, a matter of "pure grace," but something rather more complicated.[10] By contrast, in communion without baptism there is no equivalent of the parents and sponsors in baptism, who make the assent of faith and the promise to ensure that the child they present will grow up in the Christian faith and life. There is no assurance that the unbaptized communicant will be brought up in the Christian faith, no nurturing household of committed believers, and no promise by sponsors to see that the person lives into the body of Christ.

A different line of argument proposes that, rather than changing the norm of baptism-before-communion to communion-before-baptism, the church should keep the current norm while largely ignoring it. Individual congregations might, in this view, make "a conscious departure," not out of "disobedience or lack of faith," but out of a principled desire to enable "the free movement of God's grace." The communion of the unbaptized would, in this approach, be in "creative tension" with the norm.[11] In the context of the Episcopal Church, this would mean allowing congregations to depart from the canons, rather than changing the canons themselves. The problem with this approach is as much ecclesiological as it is sacramental, in how we relate to the canons and to one another within the church. The Episcopal Church's canons are, in effect, the rules by which the church has agreed to live. Neither a congregation nor even a bishop is free to contravene those canons. One might interpret silences or ambiguities in the most favorable way possible, one might advocate for the change of the canons, but one ought not flout them. When individual congregations, acting as a body, depart from the national church's canons in a matter of such importance, a congregational polity is being substituted in place of the episcopal polity of the church.

Few would argue that God cannot work through communion of the unbaptized to convey grace to the recipient, if God should so choose. Apart from the obvious foolishness of any assertion that God cannot work outside of ecclesial sequences—the Acts of the Apostles provides sufficient evidence that the Spirit could be conveyed before, during, or after baptism—there is abundant testimony from those who have participated at the table before being baptized. Sara Miles, the journalist-activist who founded the food pantry at St. Gregory of Nyssa in San Francisco, was baptized during her second year of attending the church and participating in the eucharist there, in the same week that she opened St Gregory's food pantry.[12] The unconventional sequence can "work" in the lives of individuals, considered subjectively. But the argument about communion-before-baptism really is about norms, not exceptions. It is about where the boundaries are set.

It is important to clarify exactly what sort of boundary is contemplated. While in the distant past a number of denominations used tokens or similar measures to verify who was to be admitted to receive communion at a given celebration, few do so now. No one in the Episcopal Church today is advocating a return to communion tokens or any other means of checking identity papers at the altar. There is a tradition in pastoral practice in the West not to scrutinize too closely the status of those who come forward for communion (one is instead to speak with them after the fact, if there is reason for concern). Certainly, one does not do well to repel persons from communion without advance warning. As James Farwell more pungently put it, "no pastor in her right mind will deny communion to someone who has, in fact, arrived at the altar rail expecting to receive."[13]

The "exclusion" at issue is more likely to be expressed in announcements and invitations to communion that frame it as being for the baptized, rather than snatching the host out of "unworthy" hands. The argument from hospitality is therefore a bit misplaced.

If many of the arguments advanced by advocates of communion-before-baptism are framed largely around present-day concerns, a final line of argument is more particular to the context in which Jesus operated, and it depends on a certain reading of the gospels. Jesus, it is claimed, dined with outcasts and sinners as a prophetic sign-act, designed to communicate the expansive love of God, which required no prerequisites or preconditions. Norman Perrin interpreted the meals Jesus shared with tax collectors and sinners as "an acted parable" and argued that the early Christians' communal meals were a repetition of these meals, not the Last Supper. The "table-fellowship" that Jesus shared with any and all was a foretaste of the kingdom of God, enacting a new and reconciled relationship between individuals and between the individual and God. It was this table-fellowship, Perrin argued, that most seriously offended Jesus' opponents.[14] Building on Perrin's claims, Rick Fabian, the cofounder of one of the Episcopal parishes that pioneered communion-before-baptism as a normative practice, has argued that all Christian ritual meals should re-enact this prophetic sign of persons dining together without precondition. In Fabian's view, to insist on baptism before eucharist would be to destroy the prophetic sign-act by substituting new criteria in place of Jesus' reckless generosity.[15] For Fabian, baptism should not be a prerequisite to communion but a response, as table-fellowship with Jesus caused those who were overwhelmed by his gracious hospitality to choose to commit themselves to a new life.[16] This approach, Fabian notes, mirrors the response of Zacchaeus the tax collector, who only *after* being invited to eat with Jesus responded with a change of life.[17] The meal becomes, for some but not others, the start of an initiatory process that is deepened in baptism.[18]

This argument depends on taking the totality of Jesus' meals with others as the basis or forerunner of the eucharist, rather than the traditional view, which sees the Last Supper as the basis of the eucharist. The Last Supper appears to have been a meal for the inner circle of committed disciples, while the stories of other meals in the gospels often emphasize the unexpected or unworthy folks in attendance. Indeed, Fabian goes to some lengths to dismiss the Last Supper as a model for the eucharist, arguing that we know little about it and cannot conjecture about its ritual. Therefore, he emphasizes the totality of Jesus' meal activity instead, in which he finds a clear precedent for the inclusion of the unbaptized.[19]

The evidence from scripture is more complicated than this line of argument suggests, however. Some scholars maintain the traditional view, that the eucharist is based on the Last Supper, and that this meal was different than the other meals that Jesus shared with tax collectors and prostitutes.[20] Judging from the gospel accounts, the last meal was shared not with the crowds, but with the intimate followers of Jesus—the inner circle. These same followers, minus Judas, would later be commissioned as apostles, sent to the world in his name. It was, in this analysis, a ritual meal intended to recall Jesus' vision of the kingdom of God and to commission the disciples in their ministry. The Last Supper was, therefore, a meal for the committed and initiated (the baptized) rather than a meal for all sorts and conditions of persons.[21]

Other material from scripture calls into question Fabian's portrayal of the meals Jesus shared. The persons with whom Jesus ate and drank to the scandal of others—those tax collectors and sinners—were nevertheless Jews. They already had a covenantal relationship with God. Further, Jesus was generally not the host of these other meals, quite in contrast to the Last Supper and to the way that we conceptualize the eucharist.[22] The difference in role between host and guest in the ancient world was significant, and based on the evidence one cannot speak so much of Jesus "welcoming sinners" as of him accepting the hospitality of sinners.[23] All of this complicates the picture offered by Perrin and Fabian.

If the biblical picture is somewhat ambiguous and can be interpreted in different ways, the picture from the first few generations after Jesus is far less so. It is clear that the early church very quickly interposed the bath before the meal, and the tradition of the church for twenty centuries has been clear: baptism is required before communion. In the first century, the Didache strictly stated, "No one is to eat or drink of your Eucharist but those who have been baptized in the Name of the Lord."[24] The Apology of Justin Martyr similarly insisted that only the baptized could receive.[25] The Apostolic Tradition, long attributed to Hippolytus but more likely pseudonymous and a composite of second- through fourth-century materials, also forbade giving the eucharist to an "unbeliever."[26] Any effort to admit persons to communion before baptism as the new, normative order of things must acknowledge that this is a substantial revision of the tradition.

Tradition is not the only reason defenders offer to justify the normative sequence of baptism before communion; as noted above, there is an anthropological basis for maintaining a threshold test before admitting one to fellowship. The early Christian community had strong boundaries, emerging at the very time that its sense of distinctive identity emerged, and those boundaries were maintained by limiting who came to the table.[27] Defenders of the sequence of baptism-before-communion would argue that the traditional boundary is not to be respected simply because it is old, but also—and more especially—because it is right. The early church's application of this boundary worked, both in the anthropological sense and in the theological sense.

Boundaries, however defined, help human societies form and maintain group identity. Anthropologists have found that societies use boundaries between insiders and outsiders, withhold some mysteries from noninitiates, and require instruction in a society's lore before initiation.[28] This anthropological insight is reflected in the theology of the 1979 Book of Common Prayer, which assumes a clear demarcation between the Christian life and the world.[29] The practice of communion of the unbaptized undermines this differentiation, as the merely curious are admitted to the intimate fellowship of the eucharist.

More critically, the normative sequence of baptism before communion presumes that baptism creates a relationship with God that is then nurtured in reception of the eucharist. As Leonel Mitchell has framed it, "it is through baptism that the mighty saving acts of Christ become available to us. It is birth into that new life in Christ. . . . Then the eucharist is the sacramental proclamation and celebration of that covenant relationship. . . . Baptism . . . is the basis of the relationship which the eucharist celebrates."[30] The language of the baptismal rite itself makes this clear, especially in the Thanksgiving over the Water:

We thank you, Father, for the water of Baptism. In it we are buried with Christ in his death. By it we share in his resurrection. Through it we are reborn by the Holy Spirit. Therefore in joyful obedience to your Son, we bring into his fellowship those who come to him in faith, baptizing them in the Name of the Father, and of the Son, and of the Holy Spirit.[31]

The language of rebirth is itself not insignificant, but the crucial element is the linking of baptism with entry into the fellowship of Christ. The same point is made in the post-bath ceremonies, first in the formula at the hand-laying and anointing, "N., you are sealed by the Holy Spirit in Baptism and marked as Christ's own for ever." The same concept is reiterated when the congregation welcomes the newly baptized: "We receive you into the household of God."[32] The assumption behind the liturgical texts is that baptism inaugurates an intimate relationship where before there was none.

This relationship is then nurtured in the eucharist. The eucharist itself does not purport to *create* a relationship, but rather to *foster* one that was already created in baptism. This is evident in Eucharistic Prayer C: "And so, Father, we who have been redeemed by him, and made a new people by water and the Spirit, now bring before you these gifts."[33] The eucharistic community is constituted not by the table, but by the waters of baptism. The same idea, more subtly expressed, can be found in the first of the post-communion prayers, in which the actions of font and table are paired: "Eternal God, heavenly Father, you have graciously accepted us as living members of your Son our Savior Jesus Christ, and you have fed us with spiritual food in the Sacrament of his Body and Blood."[34] The liturgical texts of the prayer book assume that baptism inaugurates a relationship that the eucharist nurtures and sustains.

Inverting the normative sequence of baptism before communion would require a substantial reordering of our ecclesiology and worship. This would include jettisoning the 1979 prayer book, or so gutting it of its baptismal ethos as to render it unrecognizable. The theology of the prayer book establishes baptism as the foundation of our ecclesiology. In the prayer book's sacramental system, once one has been baptized, the eucharist then functions as a renewal of one's baptism.

The eucharist does not and cannot on its own initiate anyone into anything, in mainstream Christian theology. Instead, baptism constitutes the Body of Christ, the church, and the eucharist is in turn the action of the whole church. This was a central insight of the Liturgical Movement of the twentieth century. It is the church as the body of Christ that gathers around the table, it is the church (with a bishop or priest as the presider) that celebrates the act of thanksgiving, and it is the church that receives the body of Christ. In this, the prayer book simply echoes the early church's understanding—from Justin Martyr, who said that the whole congregation ratified the eucharistic prayer offered in its name when it added its "Amen"; to Augustine, who told the newly baptized that, when they were given the consecrated bread and wine of the eucharist, they were to "[b]e what you can see, and receive what you are."[35] Baptism is at the heart of this, constituting the community that can celebrate the eucharist.

When proponents of communion-before-baptism assert that the eucharist can itself initiate persons into Christian fellowship, they radically reinvent both the eucharist and Christian fellowship. In their scheme, the eucharist offers membership without discipleship, identity without commitment. The result is something that bears no resemblance to a typical rite of passage, as viewed through the lens of ritual anthropology, in which there is always some cost or commitment involved in taking on a new identity and becoming a member. Indeed, because the proponents of communion-before-baptism downplay any commitment, it seems that they are not arguing for the eucharist to serve as a true initiatory rite at all: no one is initiated into anything deeper by the meal, but only to the meal itself. No one is in, no one is out, and there is no marker of identity as a Christian, because not even participation in the meal connotes allegiance, belief, or commitment.

The tradition of requiring baptism before eucharist does not spring from an anxiety about purity—a fear that the eucharist will in some way be defiled if the unwashed eat it. It is based instead on the notion that the eucharist is an action of the whole church, the body of Christ, not of individuals. One joins the body through a rite of passage—baptism—and then one continues that relationship through participation in the eucharist. To require baptism before communion is simply to insist that there is a relationship undergirding the sharing in bread and wine. That relationship could be formed when one was baptized as an infant at the initiative of the adults in one's life and then raised in the church, or it could be formed when one chose as an adult to become a Christian; in either case there exists a relationship with God through Christ. Robert MacSwain has put it more directly, writing:

> In the Episcopal Church, the eucharistic celebrant invites the congregation with the words, "The gifts of God for the People of God." This is a collective, communal invitation, rather than an individual, personal one. . . . [I]n the specific context of Christian liturgy and sacrament the term "People of God" can be reasonably understood to refer to Christians. . . . While all are invited to join the Church, the "gifts of God" are "for the People of God." To receive such gifts, to accept the invitation to the Holy Table, the altar of sacrifice, you must belong to that people.[36]

To join in the eucharist, one must first become a part of the body that celebrates the eucharist, and that happens through baptism.

Baptism, as the marker of identity, is not really exclusionary in the final sense, but rather differentiates the initiated from the not-yet-initiated. It sets a boundary, not a barrier, and boundaries serve useful functions in establishing identity. As James Farwell has remarked, based on his own pastoral experience, "newcomers do not become anxious or alienated by a clear sense of parish expectations for participation, as long as those expectations (including baptism) are presented not as the demand of law but as the invitation to life. To the contrary, newcomers become anxious and frustrated when the parish lacks a clear sense of expectation and process."[37] The anxiety about "exclusion" may be more an affliction of the well-intentioned insider than that of the guest, and the supposed remedy may be more damaging than the anxiety itself. To take up Sara Miles's metaphor of the baptismal font as a gate, when she argues against the requirement of baptism, she forgets that gates allow through-traffic, by design. The font *is* a gate, but it is a gate through which all are invited to enter, by being baptized.

Insisting on baptism before communion is based on an understanding of the proper sequence of things, not least in terms of the formation of Christians. It is not exclusionary to invite persons to come to the table by means of the font; it simply means one is invited into a process of several steps. Such a sequence pays appropriate respect to the Pauline imagery of the body of Christ (the initiated members of the church) sharing in the body of Christ (the bread and wine of the eucharist). Such a sequence also embodies what Richard Baxter taught, that one's covenant with God is renewed each time one receives communion, which amounts to a profession of faith.[38]

When this is expressed as an invitation, rather than exclusion—as an invitation to the table by way of the font—it does not appear to drive away inquirers. In my own pastoral experience, during one cycle of the catechumenate at the university church it emerged that the two catechumens preparing for baptism had, in fact, been receiving communion on occasion. In the context of a much wider discussion with each about preparation, the traditional sequence of baptism before eucharist was described. Abstention from communion as they prepared for baptism was presented as a sort of ascetical practice as well as an honoring of tradition. Both young women, without further prompting, indicated that they would henceforth come forward for a blessing rather than receive communion, until their baptism at the Easter Vigil. Neither took the conversation amiss. The obvious question, as to whether the clergy would have repelled them from communion had they put their hands forth the following Sunday, is one we did not have to resolve in the event. But there is much to be said for the value of honest, pastoral discussion of the tradition and its reasons for being. At the same time, that conversation can only happen in an overall atmosphere of hospitality and welcome.

Indeed, a colleague who converted to Christianity later in life found it quite meaningful to refrain from reception of the eucharist. For her, receiving communion was an act of intimacy—with both Christ and one's fellow believers—and therefore it required more commitment than simply showing up on a whim. That greater commitment is enacted in baptism.

Interestingly, I have known of a couple of cases of college students who had been baptized long ago but who were sponsors of catechumens preparing for baptism at the Vigil. As an ascetical exercise, and to share in the anticipation of the catechumens, these sponsors chose to abstain from receiving the eucharist during Lent. While such a practice of abstention is extraordinary and not something one might ordinarily advise, it does suggest that there are multiple ways to view the inability to receive communion before baptism.

One cannot help but wonder if the agitation to allow communion without baptism is not substituting easy communion for the harder work of evangelism, preparation, and incorporation.

The sacraments are, in the end, about relationship—they are not things to be carried about, manipulated, or possessed. This relational basis of the sacraments was one of the great insights of twentieth-century liturgical theology.[39] Inviting newcomers to the font before the table invites them into a relationship with the living God. Proponents of communion-before-baptism, who worry about exclusion when an unbaptized person is denied communion, ignore the relationship and focus on the stuff. Their approach objectifies the sacrament and reduces it to the question of whether one gets the bread and wine, as if the underlying relationship with God in Christ, which is forged in baptism, does not matter. This attitude turns the eucharist into a magic cookie, and it reflects a poor understanding of the sacraments.

COMMUNION OF ALL THE BAPTIZED

The corollary to the traditional restriction of communion to the baptized, which is to say the traditional sequence of font-to-table, is that we need to make sure that communion of the baptized is for *all* the baptized. If baptism is the action that brings one into sacramental relationship with the body of Christ, and if eucharist is the reiteration of the third and final phase of Christian initiation (baptism/chrismation/first communion), then it makes no sense to make distinctions *among* the baptized and to permit some but prohibit others to receive communion. When we insist on the sequence of font-to-table, we must also insist on the right of all the baptized, regardless of age or cognitive capacity, to receive communion. Otherwise, we make a travesty of the claim that baptism is truly full initiation into the body of Christ.

Indeed, if we bathe the new Christian without immediately feeding her, we have truncated the initiatory process. David Holeton goes so far as to argue that ancient fathers would say that the child who is baptized but not communicated is in fact not fully initiated.[40] The structure of Christian initiation is water bath, anointing (and hand-laying), and first communion, all in one unbroken liturgy.

The restoration of first communion to infant baptism is about the restoration of the integrity of Christian initiation itself. This logic is implicit in the baptismal rite of the 1979 prayer book: a candidate is baptized in water and sealed by the hand-laying (and optional chrismation). The entire liturgy is situated in the context of the eucharist, and while there is no rubric mandating that the newly baptized receive, they are singled out for duty bringing up the offerings of bread and wine, and the context of a ritual mass makes it clear that they are to receive communion.

If one accepts that baptism inaugurates a relationship with God in Christ that is then nurtured in the eucharist, to deny a baptized child the eucharist is to deny him the sacramental nourishment needed to sustain life in Christ. One cannot withhold the eucharist from the baptized without hobbling their Christian development. One does so at great peril.

This will, of course, mean the demise of so many ersatz "first communion" classes and masses. These were always anomalous: admission to communion is ritualized in baptism. Creating another liturgy to celebrate "first communion" only underscored the contradictions between our theology and practice.

Baptism brings one into the body of Christ, the church, and the eucharist is the action of that body. And this action is not just about receiving the consecrated bread and wine, but rather participating as a member of the assembly in the act of thanksgiving—so it is not enough to dismiss the children from the liturgy and later call them back just in time to receive the bread and wine. Baptized children are to take their place in the assembly and around the table precisely because they are baptized and therefore belong there. They ought not be exiled in the nursery or church school.[41] Against the objection that children will be too inattentive or too bored by the "grown-up" liturgy, it is worth recalling Aidan Kavanagh's image of children as the "coal-mine canaries" of the liturgy. Kavanagh's point is that if children show obvious signs of boredom, they are simply manifesting what the adults present are also feeling but have been socialized to conceal. The problem lies not with the children, but with the performance of the liturgy.[42]

Withholding communion from baptized children is, in fact, excommunication. In the Anglican tradition, the only legitimate basis for this is in cases of open and notorious evil, under the prayer book's disciplinary rubrics. Few children are guilty of such an offense. The dismissal of children from a portion of the liturgy is bad enough; refusing baptized children communion is worse. The practice in some places of insisting on a particular minimum age for communion is nonsensical, unless one wants to assert the same minimum age for baptism.

The eucharist is an action of the whole church, of which baptized infants are a part. When a baptized child puts out her hands for the bread, only to have her parent pull back her hand and say "no," it reflects a fundamental misunderstanding of both baptism and eucharist on the part of that parent. And if the clergy acquiesce in the parent's intervention and do not give the child communion anyway, then the clergy and parent have colluded to deny the child what is hers by right in baptism. Neither her parent nor the clergy have the right to deny that child the consecrated bread and wine. It is the right of the baptized—regardless of age—to participate in the eucharist.

The traditional objections to the communion of baptized children—that they were not yet confirmed, and that they needed instruction leading to understanding—simply have not withstood scrutiny. Baptism is now seen as full and complete initiation; confirmation is no longer a prerequisite for reception of the eucharist. The assertion that children must "understand" the eucharist before receiving had its origins not in early Christian practice, but in the catechetical program of the sixteenth-century reformers. It substitutes an educational agenda for a sacramental one, and it wrongly implies that "rational understanding must precede the reception of God's grace."[43] It also begs the question of whether most *adult* communicants actually understand communion in terms that much more advanced than the average child, and whether that understanding is likely to be accurate. How, in short, does one test for knowledge of what is fundamentally a mystery? Lee Mitchell noted pungently that an understanding of nutrition is not required before a small child is allowed to eat at the family dinner table, and by extension, he argued, one ought not insist on theological understanding of the sacrament before communion.[44] The fight over the theology of communion of baptized children was fought and won in the 1970s and 1980s.

Indeed, infant communion was not a twentieth-century innovation at all, but rather an ancient practice. Circumstantial evidence suggests that infants received communion at their baptisms in the second century, and there is clear evidence of infant communion as an accepted practice by the mid-third century in North Africa.[45] A fourth-century inscription in Sicily recorded that an eighteen-month-old received the eucharist, and the fourth-century *Apostolic Constitutions* referred to babes in arms taking the bread and wine as well.[46] A seventh-century liturgical text, the *Ordo Romanus XI*, and a twelfth-century Roman pontifical both gave instructions presuming that nursing infants would receive communion. Their only regulation was to advise that they not be nursed or receive food before receiving, and to require that infants "during the whole of Easter week . . . come to mass, offer, and receive communion every day."[47] The Gregorian Sacramentary required explicitly that infants be communicated immediately after their baptisms, and Elfric of York ordered his clergy to give newly baptized infants the eucharist.[48] The withdrawal of communion from infants happened in two stages in the eleventh and twelfth centuries, and it had nothing to do with knowledge or confirmation. It had to do with scrupulosity about the consecrated bread, if the infant could not fully swallow it. Consequently, by the twelfth century infants came to be given the cup only. When the practice of giving the laity the consecrated wine gradually ceased over the course of the eleventh and twelfth centuries, it had the incidental effect of eliminating the one kind in which infants received. Only later, in the thirteenth century, did pious traditions arise about the need to have reached the age of discretion before communion, but this was not the cause of the end of infant communion.[49] That the early church administered communion to infants was recognized in the sixteenth- and seventeenth-century debates in England between those who practiced infant baptism and those who insisted on believer's baptism. Jeremy Taylor even argued that infants should be given both sacraments or none, and infant communion was practiced in the eighteenth century by the Nonjurors, as part of their recovery of ancient liturgical practices.[50] What the Episcopal Church has done, then, is begin to recover an ancient practice, in place of a late medieval innovation, and it has done so with some Anglican precedent. This is not to say that the church has done this as a sort of antiquarian exercise, but rather that the supposed novelty of infant communion is really no novelty at all.

In some ways, the early church's example is a powerful one precisely because of the present circumstances. The post-Christendom context in which we find ourselves bears a remarkable resemblance to the situation of the church before Constantine, in that the culture no longer can be said to be working to promote the Christian life. The Christian community is now a smaller circle, defined as the assembly of the baptized that gathers around the altar. Children are part of the community; therefore they must be fully a part of that gathering.[51] Paired with this is a recovery of the biblical idea that salvation is corporate, not just individual, in that it is offered as a gift to the people of God as the community of faith. In that context, the full participation of children in the sacramental life of the community becomes an important symbol.[52] As the church has faced its new context, the experience of the early church has become, if anything, more relevant.

There are no practical or logistical challenges to the communion of infants. Very small children who have been weaned can easily handle a small bit of leavened bread or a fragment of a wafer, though care should be taken not to give bread made with honey to infants younger than one year of age, due to the risk of botulism associated with the consumption of honey, even in baked goods.[53] Infants who have not been weaned can receive a drop of wine from the smallest finger of the priest or chalice bearer (that finger does not generally touch the bread at distribution). All the baptized should receive communion on every Sunday as their baptismal right, which has nothing to do with parental desires or cognitive capacity of children.

As children participate in the eucharist, from the day of their baptism onwards, they are formed as Christians. Sharing in the liturgy and receiving communion allows experiential learning. This kind of learning is especially suited to children, of course—it is the primary basis of how the very young explore their world, begin to make associations, and learn.[54] Through the rest of early childhood, experience is an important means of learning. Indeed, theorists and practitioners of early childhood education have come to emphasize the important role of experiential learning, including taking part in adult activities. Attending the liturgy with a parent or guardian, participating in the ways that they can (singing, following along in the prayer book or hymnal, making the responses), receiving communion all help a child learn about Christian life.

Taking part in such play-based experiential education as Catechesis of the Good Shepherd or Godly Play can be a very important part of a young child's development. But playing church is not a substitute for the real thing—children should take part in both. This may mean that parents spend a great deal of time in motion: rocking a fussing infant to soothe her; taking a rambunctious toddler to the narthex to calm down, then bringing him back in, only to repeat the process again. The days of uninterrupted parental worship may well be over, until the child reaches elementary school. But this is hardly the greatest imposition that children pose on the serenity of their parents, and as with the other aspects of childrearing, the investment of parental time and energy pays dividends. And we do well to remember that children often learn by being stretched a little bit: with a more experienced peer or an adult in a collaborative context, they can advance in their development.[55] With a parent or other adult guiding them, the liturgy can open up for small children. At the same time, the child's wonderment, occasional exclamation, and spontaneous discovery can open up the liturgy for the adult who is with him.

Parents will rarely be able to keep a very young child from making any noise or from squirming a little. Preschool and elementary-age children can be expected to do a bit better. Soft toys, crayons, and other quiet diversions can help, and it helps to sit with a view of the action. Children often do better in the front of the church (perhaps on a side aisle for a quick escape if needed), where they are able to watch the action, rather than in the back. Most parents are quite sensitized to their own children's misbehavior and will remove an unruly child before others are seriously affected. Those who need their public worship to be entirely free of even occasional, mild disruptions may need to ponder whether they may, in fact, have a monastic vocation. Withdrawal from the world into a cloister may be the only way for such delicate souls to ensure the contemplative silence they crave. The parish liturgy is, like it or not, the action of the whole church, which necessarily includes all generations.

Full participation in the eucharist, in addition to being the birthright of all the baptized, is also an important, even crucial, part of a child's upbringing in the Christian faith and life. Logistical concerns and fears of misbehavior are not legitimate reasons for the excommunication of infants and small children. And children should not be exiled out of the assembly for any part of the liturgy to some "children's chapel" or Sunday school. All the baptized belong in the liturgical assembly together.

When my son, Will, was baptized at the Easter Vigil in 2009, he also received communion. He was eight-and-a-half months old, and I communicated him by dipping a small piece of (leavened) bread into the chalice and then feeding it to him (even younger children can be communicated by means of a spoon or by a little finger dipped in the wine and offered to the child to suck). Was Will able to understand the meaning of the sacrament? He knew it was food, and he seemed to have perceived that it was a special occasion. He heard the singing of the choir during the communion anthem, and he looked around at all of the flurry of activity at the altar—the bishop, in his robes, passing out bread, and the swirling dance of chalice bearers circling the altar to administer the wine—and he smiled. Could he discourse about the nature of Christ's presence in the bread and wine? Of course not. But just as I would not deny him physical nourishment, so I would not deny him the spiritual nourishment to which his baptism entitles him. Since that day, Will has continued to participate in the eucharist by attending the "grown-up" liturgy and receiving the consecrated bread and wine. He has come to participate more fully over time, and he knows more of the significance of the eucharist. As we wait our turn to go up to the altar to receive communion, he talks with anticipation about the bread and wine, and not in the way he speaks of ordinary food. I know that as he grows in years, he will continue to grow in understanding of the sacrament. He, like his father, will likely never "understand" it fully, for it is a mystery, but he will share in that sense of the thing that we are allowed to have, this side of the grave.

Notes

1. BCP 1979, 304.

2. Kathryn Tanner, "In Praise of Open Communion: A Rejoinder to James Farwell," *Anglican Theological Review* 86 (2004): 481.

3. Sara Miles, *Take This Bread: A Radical Conversion* (New York: Ballantine Books, 2007), 79.

4. Tanner, "In Praise of Open Communion," 482–83; Stephen Edmondson, "Opening the Table: The Body of Christ and God's Prodigal Grace," *Anglican Theological Review* 91 (2009): 218–19.

5. Edmondson, "Opening the Table," 222.

6. See also Galatians 4:4–7.

7. James Farwell, "Baptism, Eucharist, and the Hospitality of Jesus: On the Practice of 'Open Communion,'" *Anglican Theological Review* 86 (2004): 237. For a discussion of work on symbolic boundaries and identity, see Michèle Lamont and Virág Molnár, "The Study of Boundaries in the Social Sciences," *Annual Review of Sociology* 28 (2002): 167–95.

8. Edmondson, "Opening the Table," 230.

9. Kavanagh, *Shape of Baptism*, 108–10.

10. James Farwell, "A Brief Reflection on Kathryn Tanner's Response to 'Baptism, Eucharist, and the Hospitality of Jesus,'" *Anglican Theological Review* 87 (2005): 308.

11. Mark W. Stamm, *Let Every Soul Be Jesus' Guest: A Theology of the Open Table* (Nashville, TN: Abingdon Press, 2006), 10–11, 13, 19, 39.

12. Miles, *Take This Bread*, 119–21.

13. Farwell, "Baptism, Eucharist, and the Hospitality of Jesus," 217.

14. Norman Perrin, *Rediscovering the Teaching of Jesus* (London: Harper & Row, 1967), 103–07, 121.

15. Richard Fabian, "Patterning the Sacraments after Christ," *OPEN: The Journal of the Associated Parishes for Liturgy and Mission* 40 (1994): 1–2; Richard Fabian, "The Scandalous Table," unpublished paper (2010): 9–10. I am grateful to Rick Fabian for sharing his typescript with me.

16. Fabian, "Patterning the Sacraments after Christ," 4; Mark Stamm underscores the argument that Jesus' meals were initiatory (Stamm, *Let Every Soul Be Jesus' Guest*, 41–43).

17. Richard Fabian, "First the Table, Then the Font," *http://www.saintgregorys.org/Resources_pdfs/FirsttheTable.pdf*, accessed June 20, 2008.

18. Edmondson, "Opening the Table," 230–31.

19. Fabian, "Scandalous Table," 21–22.

20. For example, John Koenig, *The Feast of the World's Redemption: Eucharistic Origins and Christian Mission* (Harrisburg, PA: Trinity Press International, 2000); Enrico Mazza, *The Celebration of the Eucharist: The Origin of the Rite and the Development of Its Interpretation*

(Collegeville, MN: The Liturgical Press, 1999), 19–34. But compare Andrew McGowan, who argues, "the history of the Eucharist proper begins after [Jesus]." Andrew McGowan, "Rethinking Eucharistic Origins," *Pacifica* 23 (2010): 183. For McGowan, the speculations of both Koenig on the one side and Fabian and Perrin on the other are misplaced.

21. Farwell, "Baptism, Eucharist, and the Hospitality of Jesus," 220–22. But Donald Schell challenges the common view that the Last Supper was a meal with disciples only, asserting that it was just as open as all of the other meals Jesus shared. Donald Schell, "Baptizing Those Already Welcomed to Jesus' Table," *http://www.allsaintscompany.org/resources/view/baptizing_those_already_welcomed_to_jesus_table*, accessed June 20, 2008.

22. A point made by the Theology Committee of the House of Bishops of the Episcopal Church, "Reflections on Holy Baptism and the Holy Eucharist: A Response to Resolution D084 of the 75th General Convention," *Anglican Theological Review* webpage: 4–5. *http://anglicantheologicalreview.org/static/pdf/articles/House_of_Bishops_on_Open_Table.pdf*, accessed August 7, 2012.

23. Andrew McGowan, "Whose Meal Is It Anyway? Jesus, the Church and Eucharistic Origins: The Barry Marshall Memorial Lecture, Trinity College," *Trinity Papers* 24 (June 2003): 7. *http://www.trinity.unimelb.edu.au/Media/docs/TrinityPaper24-0022b068-a672-47dd-a8de-45-a55288fcda-0.pdf*, accessed August 19, 2012.

24. "The Didache," 2.9, in *Early Christian Writings*, trans. Maxwell Staniforth and Andrew Louth (London: Penguin, 1987), 195.

25. Justin Martyr, "The First Apology" in *The Ante-Nicene Fathers: Translations of the Writings of the Fathers down to A.D. 325*, ed. Alexander Roberts and James Donaldson, vol. 1 (Grand Rapids, MI: Wm. B. Eerdman's, 1956), 185.

26. Bradshaw, Johnson, and Phillips, *Apostolic Tradition*, 37, 182–83; see also pages 4–6 on authorship and dating; also Paul F. Bradshaw, *The Search for the Origins of Christian Worship: Sources and Methods for the Study of Early Liturgy*, 2nd ed. (Oxford: Oxford University Press, 2002), 82–83.

27. Koenig, *Feast of the World's Redemption*, 111; Wayne A. Meeks, *The First Urban Christians: The Social World of the Apostle Paul* (New Haven, CT: Yale University Press, 1983), 190; McGowan, "Whose Meal Is It Anyway?," 13–14.

28. See Arnold van Gennep, *The Rites of Passage*, trans. Monika B. Vizedom and Gabrielle L. Caffee (Chicago: University of Chicago Press, 1960); Victor Turner, *The Ritual Process: Structure and Anti-Structure* (New York: Aldine de Gruyter, 1969), 94–130.

29. Farwell, "Baptism, Eucharist, and the Hospitality of Jesus," 228.

30. Leonel L. Mitchell, "Should the Unbaptized Be Welcomed to the Lord's Table?" *Open* (Fall 1994): 5–6.

31. BCP 1979, 306–7.

32. BCP 1979, 308.

33. BCP 1979, 371; also Theology Committee, "Reflections on Holy Baptism and the Holy Eucharist," 3.

34. BCP 1979, 365.

35. Justin Martyr, "The First Apology," in Roberts and Donaldson, eds., *The Ante-Nicene Fathers*, 186; Augustine, "Sermon 272: On the Day of Pentecost to the *Infantes*, on the Sacrament," in John E. Rotelle, O.S.A., ed., *The Works of Saint Augustine*, part III, vol. 7 *Sermons*, trans. Edmund Hill, O.P. (New Rochelle, NY: New City Press, 1993), 301.

36. Robert MacSwain, "'The Gifts of God for the People of God': Some Thoughts on Baptism and Eucharist" *Sewanee Theological Review* 56 (2012): 83. Emphasis in the original.

37. Farwell, "Baptism, Eucharist, and the Hospitality of Jesus," 237.

38. Richard Baxter, *A Petition for Peace: With the Reformation of the Liturgy* (London: n.p., 1661), 48; Richard Baxter, *Confirmation and Restauration* (London: Printed by A. M. for Nevil Simmons book-seller in Kederminster, and are to be sold by Joseph Cranford, at the Kings-Head in Pauls Church-yard, 1658), 150.

39. Odo Casel, *The Mystery of Christian Worship*, ed. Burkhard Neunheuser (Westminster, MD: Newman Press, 1962); Edward Schillebeeckx, *Christ the Sacrament of the Encounter with God* (New York: Sheed and Ward, 1963).

40. David R. Holeton, *Infant Communion—Then and Now* (Bramcote, Nottingham: Grove Books, 1981), 22.

41. Taft makes the point that baptized children are called to *participation*, not just *reception*. Taft, "On the Question of Infant Communion," 208.

42. Aidan Kavanagh, *Elements of Rite*, 67–68.

43. Louis Weil, "Disputed Aspects of Infant Communion" in Ruth Meyers, ed., *Children at the Table: The Communion of All the Baptized in Anglicanism Today* (New York: Church Hymnal Corp., 1995), 190–91.

44. Leonel L. Mitchell, "Communion of Infants and Little Children," *Anglican Theological Review* 71 (1989): 72.

45. Ruth A. Meyers, "Infant Communion: Reflections on the Case from Tradition," *Anglican and Episcopal History* 57 (1988): 160–62; Holeton, *Infant Communion*, 4.

46. Mark Dalby, *Infant Communion: The New Testament to the Reformation* (Cambridge: Grove Books, 2003), 11–12; Holeton, *Infant Communion*, 5.

47. Quoted in Taft, "On the Question of Infant Communion," 208–9.

48. Dalby, *Infant Communion*, 17–18.

49. Taft, "On the Question of Infant Communion," 209; Meyers, "Infant Communion," 163–64; Fisher, *Christian Initiation*, 101–8; Dalby, *Infant Communion*, 21–22, 25.

50. David R. Holeton, "Communion of All the Baptized and Anglican Tradition," *Anglican Theological Review* 69 (1987): 20–24.

51. Holeton, *Infant Communion*, 24.

52. Weil, "Disputed Aspects of Infant Communion," 192.

53. This is due to the risk of botulism associated with the consumption of honey, which can contain the spores of the bacterium (up to 13 percent of honey samples do). The spores are not destroyed by baking, and in the immature digestive system of a child under one year of age, the spores activate and produce a potent toxin. If a parish uses a recipe for leavened bread containing honey, one might use wafers for infants, in the same way that many parishes consecrate gluten-free wafers alongside leavened wheat bread to accommodate those with celiac disease. It would be preferable, though, to use a recipe without honey or to substitute a different sweetener. Haim M. Solomon and Timothy Lilly Jr., "Bacteriological Analytical Manual: Chapter 17: *Clostridium botulinum*," *http://www.fda.gov/Food/ScienceResearch/Laboratory Methods/BacteriologicalAnalyticalManualBAM/ucm070879.htm*, accessed August 5, 2012; James P. Smith, Daphne Phillips Daifas, Wassim El-Khoury, and John W. Austin, "Microbial Safety of Bakery Products," in *Microbial Safety of Minimally Processed Foods*, ed. John S. Novak, Gerald M. Sapers, and Vijay K. Juneja (Boca Raton, FL: CRC Press, 2003), 18–20.

54. See, for example, McDevitt and Ormrod, *Child Development*, 141–43, 154–58.

55. This is Lev Vygotsky's concept of a "zone of proximal development"—the skills or competencies that lie beyond what a child can achieve on his own, but can be achieved in collaboration with an adult or a more experienced peer through a process of "scaffolding." See, for example, McDevitt and Ormrod, *Child Development*, 164–66, 169–71, 174–76, 179–80.

Epilogue

INITIATION THAT WORKS

What does Christian initiation look like, when properly done?

Candidates are carefully prepared. The parish adopts the approach of the catechumenate, both for the unbaptized candidate seeking to go to the font and for the person preparing to make a mature, public reaffirmation of his or her baptismal vows. The *Book of Occasional Services 2003* makes a clear distinction between catechumens (unbaptized adults) and baptized persons who are preparing to reaffirm their baptismal vows, by separating them into two different processes. Some parishes that use the catechumenate do not make such a division. Whether the BOS's parallel processes are used or only a single process, parishes are careful not to confuse the baptized and the unbaptized. The catechumenate's emphasis on formation over information, on walking the walk of Christian life, and on the creation of supportive community in small groups and in sponsoring relationships works effectively for those seeking to reaffirm their vows as well as for those making their vows for the first time.

The whole community is involved. The Roman Catholic Rite of Christian Initiation of Adults appropriately insisted that the catechumens are an integral part of the parish community and that they are appropriately the subject of the care and concern of the entire liturgical assembly, not just those involved formally in the catechumenate as catechists or sponsors. The Episcopal Church's *Book of Occasional Services* did underscore that catechumens are to be considered a part of the community from the time of their admission, but the BOS did not include RCIA's insistence on the involvement of the entire parish community, which is a loss. While some laity will be involved in particular roles, as catechists and sponsors, the entire assembly should be asked, in the liturgy, to pray for the catechumens, and ways should be found to encourage the faithful to show their support for the catechumens.

At baptism, all candidates are chrismated at the consignation (the "sealing"). The 1979 prayer book allows the use of chrism on an optional basis, but the restoration of chrism was a crucial element in the restoration of the ancient church's unitary rite of initiation. The use of chrism should be normative, to make clear the restoration of the ancient church's baptismal rite.

The symbols of baptism (water, oil, etc.) are used extravagantly and abundantly. Symbols work best when they are big. Water is the crucial symbol in baptism, and so the celebrant should pay careful attention to the way it is used. The New Testament texts speak of one being buried in the baptismal waters before being raised in Jesus Christ, and the imagery of drowning is frequent in Christian writings. While it is theoretically possible to drown in a small quantity of water, for most humans water acquires the element of danger only when there is quite a bit present. For standing fonts, the rule of thumb I tell my students is this: if there isn't enough water to drown someone, there isn't enough water. Immersion fonts are to be preferred, for obvious reasons. If Episcopalians can't get over the fact that other groups, such as the Southern Baptists, immerse candidates, then perhaps we need to ask ourselves to what degree denominational snobbery is evidence of the sin of pride.

Oil, in chrismation, should be fragrant, slick, and all over the candidate. The liturgical cotton ball that occasionally rears its head in the celebration of baptism, held captive in a small, thimble-sized oil stock until it moistens (barely) the celebrant's thumb, bears as much resemblance to the kingly/prophetic anointing that chrismation is supposed to recall as a shot glass of Welch's grape juice bears to a nice glass of Shiraz. A small oil stock and the grudging distribution of chrism do not communicate what the symbol is meant to convey. The celebrant should *pour* oil directly from the vessel onto the candidate's head and then trace the cross; or failing that, the celebrant could pour a quantity of oil onto his/her cupped hand, smear that on the forehead of the candidate, and then trace the cross.

The parish, the diocese, and the national church treat the newly baptized, regardless of age, as full members of the church. The prayer book has insisted, since 1979, that baptism is "full initiation by water and the Holy Spirit into Christ's Body the Church." Thirty-three years and eleven subsequent General Conventions later, the church has not yet brought its canons into full conformity with this theological tenet. Resolutions to amend the canons governing various lay positions in the church as well as the ordination canons, to remove the requirement of confirmation, were derailed in 2012. The result is that ordinands are still required to be confirmed (III.6.2, III.8.2), as is the chancellor to the Presiding Bishop (I.2.5), members of Executive Council (I.4.2(c)) and standing commissions (I.1.2(a)), and (in ordinary circumstances) licensed lay ministers of varying types (III.4.1(a)). It is difficult, in light of these canonical provisions, to believe that the church really means what it says when it affirms baptism as "full initiation," since clearly an additional step was required of those called to particular forms of service. The canons should be changed to reflect the theology of the church: confirmation adds nothing to baptism, and therefore it should not serve as the prerequisite for anything.

Those who are baptized receive communion at the eucharist in their baptismal liturgy, and at every liturgical celebration thereafter at which they are present. More than any other practice in the church's treatment of the baptized, the withholding of communion from baptized persons is an affront to the theology of the prayer book. Christian initiation was, anciently, a three-part liturgy: baptism, hand-laying, first communion. Arguably, any baptism at which the candidate does not receive communion is a mutilated liturgy. Baptism is full initiation, and that means that all the baptized, regardless of age, are entitled to share in the eucharistic banquet. Baptismal rights have nothing to do with cognition, but those who would withhold communion from children until they "understand" the sacrament ignore both extensive research on human development and considerable material on the religious understanding of small children. More importantly, they confuse God's gracious action by making it depend on human intellectual capacity. All baptized persons, including infants and children, should be given the body and blood in the consecrated bread and wine.

There will be an optional, repeatable rite of reaffirmation of baptismal vows. There is great pastoral wisdom in providing a rite by which one might reaffirm baptismal vows. The 1979 prayer book provides just such a rite of reaffirmation. The name of "confirmation" threatens to introduce theological confusions largely because of its history, implying that baptism is insufficient on its own. The church might consider eliminating the categories of "confirmation" and "reception," allowing the use of the rite of reaffirmation in all circumstances in which it seems pastorally appropriate for baptized persons to make a public affirmation of faith—whether at a transition from one faith community or denomination to another, or at a particular watershed in one's life or development. This would remove theological confusion and underscore that baptism is full initiation into Christ's body, the church. But if this is thought too radical, the church can at least make clear in its practice and in its teaching that confirmation/reception/reaffirmation is simply a reaffirmation of baptismal vows. Above all, we need to make it clear that this rite of reaffirmation is *optional*, to be undertaken if and when the individual's circumstances and faith-journey warrant it. If holy baptism is, in fact, full initiation by water and the Spirit—and we assert in the prayer book that it is—then we must stop expecting the baptized to jump through another ritual hoop later on.

By reforming our initiatory processes and rituals, we can move closer to the vision of Christian initiation that the early church's documents present, and the vision of the active, informed participation of the laity in the liturgy that was the goal of the Liturgical Movement of the twentieth century, which produced the 1979 prayer book. But more importantly, the reform of our initiatory practices is one of the best steps we can take to revivify the church, by placing its focus on the mission of inviting others into a new relationship with the Lord of life, welcoming them into the fellowship of believers, equipping them to live lives of integrity and self-sacrifice, and then commissioning them for service to the world in Christ's name, bringing God's reconciling love to all persons that they encounter in their lives. Christian initiation is about all of those things: inviting, welcoming, training, encouraging, commissioning, and sending forth. That we rarely hear or see it described as such in our parish churches is a sign of how far we are from the ideal of the 1979 prayer book, and from the example of the early church.

This is a point worth underscoring: the Liturgical Movement that produced the 1979 prayer book in the Episcopal Church, and that produced the revised rites of the Roman Catholic Church, the churches that came to form the Evangelical Lutheran Church in America, and other bodies, was not about antiquarianism. When early church documents and liturgies were cited, it was not the pursuit of the past for the past's sake. That movement was marked by a sincere conviction that liturgy matters, and that changing the liturgy to promote the active, informed, meaningful participation of the whole people of God went hand-in-hand with larger changes in church life. All of those changes were intended to bring people into relationship with God through Christ, and to deepen their engagement once they were initiated into the Christian life.

This is urgent work. It is quite possible that mainline Christianity will fade away, and the Episcopal Church with it. This will not come because we are too lax in our approach to the Bible, nor because we have decided, as a denomination, to take the costly step of welcoming those who live or love or look differently than we do. If the Episcopal Church does die out, it will be because we were too afraid to live into the baptismal covenant of the 1979 prayer book, and too embarrassed to bring new people into an encounter with the Lord who lies behind it. The cheap grace that some accuse the Episcopal Church of peddling lies not in those congregations that have embraced the fundamental worth and dignity of women or gay folk or ethnic minorities or the poor—a worth and dignity indicated by the baptismal covenant's promise to seek and serve Christ in all persons and to respect the dignity of every human being. Where cheap grace is peddled, it is in those places that do not use the 1979 baptismal covenant, or do not take it seriously; in those places where baptism happens willy-nilly and without catechumenal preparation; in those places where Christian faith in the Episcopal tradition is regarded more like a fraternity or a social club and less the Way of the one who hung out with sinners and ate with them.

This book has urged a handful of things: a revived catechumenate, operating in each parish; a religious community that makes each new person the object of its concern and prayer; a liturgical leader who uses appropriate symbols well; a national church that cleans up its canons and texts to clarify that it meant what it said when it stated that baptism is full initiation into Christ's body, the church; and an appropriate seriousness about baptism as the transition to an entirely new way of life, with spine-chilling promises that we seek to live into over the space of a lifetime, encouraged and supported by our fellow-travelers.

Ritual matters. It forms us on deep levels, levels of cognition that often escape easy verbalization. By transforming our ritual, we can, in turn, be transformed as disciples. Changing the liturgy is not a panacea, and merely changing the baptismal and confirmation practices of the Episcopal Church will not cure all ills. But recapturing the vision of the life of the baptized, and of the ministry of the whole people of God, will in turn better shape us as disciples, so that we can then get on with the business of living out our baptismal calling in the world around us.

CPSIA information can be obtained
at www.ICGtesting.com
Printed in the USA
FFOW01n0122160917
39893FF